A GUIDE TO
FRESHWATER
INVERTEBRATE
ANIMALS

by
T. T. MACAN
M.A., PH.D.

LONGMAN

LONGMAN GROUP LIMITED
London

*Associated companies, branches and representatives
throughout the world*

First published 1959
Sixth impression 1970
Seventh impression 1972

ISBN 0 582 32274 X

*Printed in Hong Kong by
Wing Tai Cheung Printing Co Ltd*

A GUIDE TO
FRESHWATER
INVERTEBRATE
ANIMALS

CONTENTS

INTRODUCTION

IT is not possible in our present state of knowledge to write a book by means of which every species of aquatic animal may be named. For one thing, many are the immature stages of insects of which only the adults can be identified, though probably there are good differences between the larvae and nymphs waiting to be described. Furthermore, some of the groups in which adults are aquatic have not been studied properly for a long time.

The object of the present work is to enable collectors to identify their captures to the nearest group, and references are given, where possible, whereby those who wish may identify the species. At first sight the writer's idea of the "nearest group" will appear illogical and capricious, but it is believed that this impression will disappear with familiarity with fresh-water animals; for example, all naturalists will know by its specific name a unique and distinct creature like *Nepa cinerea*, the Water Scorpion (fig. 196), but most, unless they be specialists in the group, will be satisfied if they can assign a member of the little-known and difficult Oligochaeta (worms) to the proper family. It must, however, be admitted that the microscopic animals have been treated more sketchily than the larger ones.

An attempt has been made to cater for the amateur naturalist and for the professional biologist. The latter is asked to bear patiently with expositions of simple points and the former with what may seem an excessive number of technical references.

The most satisfactory form for an undertaking of this sort appears to be a key, and, since this may not be familiar to every reader, a description of how a key works is appropriate at this point.

The numbers in the left-hand margin run serially, and against each stands a pair of questions. The observer, having examined his specimen, decides which of the alternatives applies to the specimen, and then finds that opposite to it there is a number in the right-hand margin. This is the number of the next pair of questions to be answered, and so it goes on until eventually, instead of a number in the right-hand margin, there is a name in heavy type—the name of the specimen or the group to which it belongs. A name in small capitals followed by a number is the name of a higher group which is split up further on in the key. It is undesirable to overburden a key with names of this kind, but the inclusion of the most important seems desirable.

The Animal Kingdom is divided into a series of main groups or phyla, and successive divisions are Classes, Orders and Families, with various intermediate grades which have been ignored here. Sometimes animals do not fall obviously into these groups and different authors arrange them in different ways. Further, it often happens that, though two authors agree on what animals belong to a given group, one may call it a class, for example, and the other something higher or lower in the series. Families and sub-families comprise genera and species. Every organism is commonly referred to by its generic and trivial or species name. The final answer is always printed in heavy type. If an identification is to the species, that fact is evident from the two names followed by that of the author— i.e. the person who originally described the species. Families and sub-families are recognized by the terminations -idae and -inae respectively. Any other solitary name is the name of the genus. When higher groups are indicated, "Order", "Class" or whatever it may be is inserted before the name. Alternative names are placed in brackets; it is, unfortunately, imperative to quote a certain number, in order that readers may turn to other books and not be confused.

But, having decided to use the key form, I have not felt obliged to stick slavishly to it throughout. Sometimes, especially at the highest levels, it is difficult to find clear-cut distinctions which do not require extensive qualification. An example occurs at once; radial symmetry is characteristic of the Coelenterata, and the tentacles radiating round the mouth of most of them render this character immediately apparent. But one genus has no tentacles, and the radial symmetry is therefore far from apparent. Where a cursive account has seemed more convenient it has been used. In the author's experience, it is more disheartening to arrive at an obviously wrong answer in a small key than in a big one, and accordingly in the following pages what is in fact one long continuous key has been broken up into several.

References to works by which the reader can take identification farther are included at the appropriate places. The contractions are those used in *The World List of Scientific Periodicals*, but certain series which are devoted entirely to taxonomy and which are referred to frequently, are indicated by initials only, as follows:

F.B.A.S.P.	Scientific Publications of the Freshwater Biological Association.
R.S.	Ray Society's Monographs.
L.S.S.B.F.	Linnean Society's Synopses of the British Fauna.
S.W.F.D.	Süsswasserfauna Deutschlands.
T.W.D.	Tierwelt Deutschlands.
T.M.E.	Tierwelt Mitteleuropas.
F.F.	Faune de France.

The references given have been used in the compilation of the keys, and extensive use has been made of Wesenberg-Lund's two volumes: *Biologie der Süsswassertiere* (Vienna: Springer, 1939) and *Biologie der Süsswasserinsekten* (Vienna: Springer, 1943); also of *Freshwater Biology* by H. B. Ward and G. C. Whipple (New York: Wiley). This latter work is, however, of limited value to students of the European fauna, since it deals exclusively with animals of North America. More extensive use would have been made of Bertrand, H., 1954, *Les insectes aquatiques d'Europe*, had it appeared earlier than it did.

The names are generally taken from the works cited, except those of insects which follow *A Check List of British Insects*, by G. S. Kloet and W. D. Hincks (Stockport, 1945).

The number of species (spp.) quoted, when possible, for each group is the number recorded in the British Isles.

It was originally planned that the work should be illustrated by Mr R. D. Cooper, but he completed only a few drawings before his untimely death. Most of the rest are by the author, and have been drawn from living specimens when possible, though it has been necessary to copy a certain number. When a live specimen is drawn in its natural position, which is often characteristic, only slight magnification is possible, and the artist is faced with the question whether to draw what he sees or whether he should subsequently kill the animal, examine it piecemeal under a microscope, and add to the drawing details of such things as small bristles and fine hairs. I have taken the view that, for present purposes, excess of detail may confuse rather than help, particularly if a reader is not equipped with a first-class microscope, and make the point in order to explain differences that readers may note between the illustrations here and those in other books. For example, *Sialis* (fig. 118) is commonly depicted with a fringe of hairs round each gill. It certainly has such hairs, but as they are difficult to see except under high magnification I have left them out.

I wish to thank Mrs J. C. Mackereth and Dr H. E. Hinton for advice on the keys to Trichoptera and Diptera respectively.

Legends to the figures

c.s. = cast skin.	l.s. = living specimen.
m.s. = mounted specimen.	p.s. = preserved specimen.

See also footnote on p. 31.

FREE-LIVING ANIMALS

Animals living permanently on the surface of or inside some other animal are treated separately on p. 112.

Key 1

1. Animals in which all the vital functions are performed by a single cell; generally one cell is an individual but sometimes a number are joined together in a colony (figs. 2 and 3); occasionally the cell may contain a number of nuclei, though there is no division of the protoplasm. All are microscopic, though the largest can just be seen with the naked eye, and it is worth noting that the largest of these single-celled animals are larger than the smallest of the many-celled animals   .   .   . Phylum PROTOZOA 2

— Animals consisting of a number of cells, some or all of which are specialized for particular functions   .   . 5

2. Cell provided with a few relatively long lashing filaments (fig. 1); most swim through the water by means of these, but a few attach themselves to the substratum; in some genera, e.g. *Volvox* (fig. 2), a number of cells are connected by a gelatinous matrix; some secrete cases, and these may be joined together to form a colony; individuals may also be connected by a simple stalk to form a colony (fig. 3). (Many members of this group are true plants;

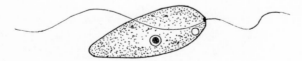

Fig. 1
Bodo obovatus Lemm. (after Pascher)

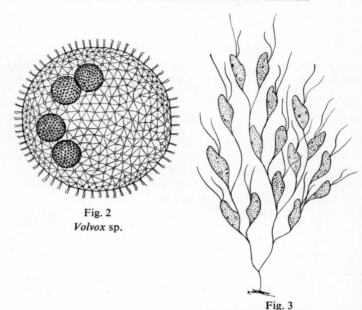

Fig. 2
Volvox sp.

Fig. 3
Dendromonas laxa (S. Kent)
Blochmann (after Pascher)

others can feed after the manner of plants or animals)
Class Flagellata (Mastigophora)

Pascher, A. (1913–1927), Flagellatae. *Süsswasserflora Deutschlands*, parts 1–4 and 11.

— Cell without long lashing filaments 3

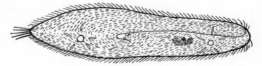

Fig. 4
Paramecium caudatum Ehrenb. (after Kahl)

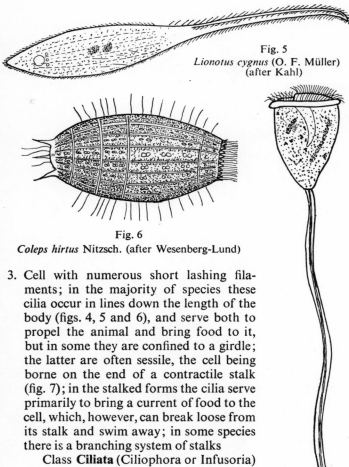

Fig. 5
Lionotus cygnus (O. F. Müller)
(after Kahl)

Fig. 6
Coleps hirtus Nitzsch. (after Wesenberg-Lund)

3. Cell with numerous short lashing filaments; in the majority of species these cilia occur in lines down the length of the body (figs. 4, 5 and 6), and serve both to propel the animal and bring food to it, but in some they are confined to a girdle; the latter are often sessile, the cell being borne on the end of a contractile stalk (fig. 7); in the stalked forms the cilia serve primarily to bring a current of food to the cell, which, however, can break loose from its stalk and swim away; in some species there is a branching system of stalks

Class **Ciliata** (Ciliophora or Infusoria)

Kahl, A. (1930–1935), T.W.D., parts 18, 21, 25 and 30.

— Cell without short lashing filaments . 4

Fig. 7
Vorticella sp.

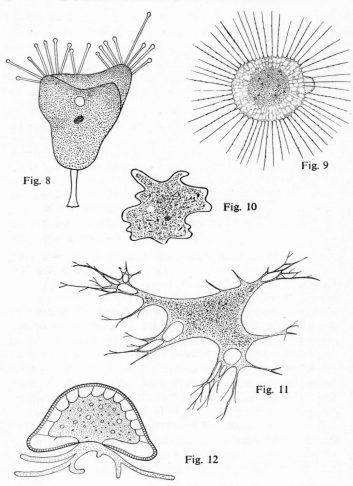

Fig. 8, A suctorian (after Wesenberg-Lund; Fig. 9, *Actinosphaerium eichhornii* (Ehrenb.) (after Cash et al.); Fig. 10, *Amoeba* sp.; Fig. 11, *Penardia mutabilis* Cash (after Cash et al.); Fig. 12, *Arcella vulgaris* Ehrenb. (after Cash et al.)

4. Generally with knobbed tentacles, and generally fixed with or without a stalk; never lacking both these characters (fig. 8) . . . . . Subclass **Suctoria**

> This group is generally included in the Ciliata because they are like them when young, but this affinity is not obvious in the adults, and they are more likely to be mistaken for Rhizopoda.

— Without knobbed tentacles and free-moving; (the characteristic features are the pseudopodia, which may be long, radiating, fine and permanent (Heliozoa or sun animalcules, fig. 9), or no more than temporary extrusions of the elastic surface (as in *Amoeba* (fig. 10)); in some they are long, fine and branching, and they may anastomose (fig. 11). Most possess cases of a chitinoid substance (fig. 12), of silica, or of sand grains picked up from the substratum (fig. 13) . . . Class **Rhizopoda** (Sarcodina)

> Cash, J., Hopkinson, J., and Wailes, G. H. (1905, 1909, 1915, 1919, 1921), *The British Freshwater Rhizopoda and Heliozoa.* R.S., 5 vols.

5. Animals consisting of a whitish or greenish encrusting growth on stones, branches and any firm submerged object. They are pierced by small holes of various sizes, and on close examination they are seen to have a texture similar to that of a bath-sponge, though much finer. They cannot be mistaken for any other animal, and, indeed, the difficulty most likely to arise is the recognition that these formless immovable objects are animals at all.

Sponges **Spongillidae** (Phylum PORIFERA)

> 5 spp. Stephens, J. (1920), *Proc. R. Irish Acad.* **35,** 205–254.

— Not forming an encrusting growth . . . 6

6. This group, the Coelenterata, familiar to anyone who knows sea-animals because sea-anemones and jellyfish belong to it, is difficult to define precisely, and at this point

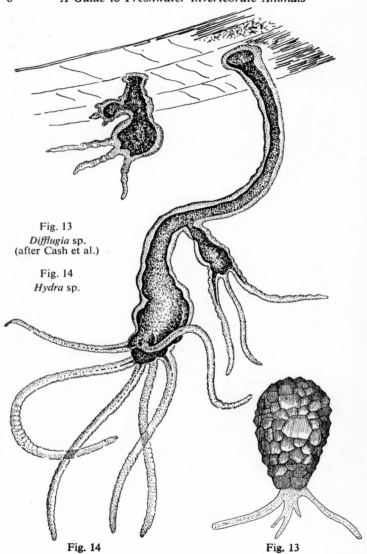

Fig. 13
Difflugia sp.
(after Cash et al.)

Fig. 14
Hydra sp.

Fig. 14   Fig. 13

it is convenient to abandon strict adherence to the dichoto-
mous key. The most familiar freshwater representatives are
Hydra (2 spp.) and *Chlorohydra* (1 sp.) which are often
found hanging from water plants and other points of
vantage, and which consist of a tubular body, sometimes
as much as 4–5 cm long when fully extended, with a
terminal opening surrounded by tentacles (fig. 14). The
radiating symmetry would be a good diagnostic character
for the whole group but for the existence of polyps which
lack tentacles and consequently appear at first sight to be
small worms. Their true status becomes apparent under the
microscope, which reveals the simple structure and also
the harpoon cells characteristic of the phylum. Two species
have been recorded from Britain: *Protohydra leuckarti*
Greef, at most 3 mm long, and club-shaped, occurs in
brackish water usually lying with the end distant from the
mouth embedded in the mud; and what used to be called
Microhydra ryderi, also very small but differing in shape in
that there is a slight constriction below the mouth so that
the polyp is flask-shaped. There is a big concentration of
harpoon cells above the constriction. It is now known,
however, that there is an alternation of generations in this
species as in most marine forms, and Microhydra is the
polyp stage of *Craspedacusta sowerbii* Lankester, a free-
swimming jellyfish up to 19 mm across, which has been
recorded a few times in British fresh waters.

Hydra can reproduce by branching at the side (fig. 14). If
conditions are good, there may be more than one bud,
sometimes up to 10. *Cordylophora* is like a *Hydra* from
which numerous buds have never become detached, but it
is easily distinguished, first because there are generally
more polyps than a reproducing *Hydra* ever has, secondly
because the tentacles do not all come off at the same level,
and thirdly because the stem secretes a thin hard tube
round itself. *Cordylophora lacustris* Allman occurs in some
of the Norfolk Broads and some East Coast estuaries.

Phylum **Coelenterata**

Ewer, R. F. (1948/9), A review of the Hydridae and two new species of *Hydra* from Natal. *Proc. zool. Soc. Lond.*, **118**, 226–244.

— Unlike any of the above-mentioned animals   .   .   7

7. Microscopic animals rarely over 2 mm long; typically with cilia at the front end which serve both for locomotion and feeding, and from which the name "wheel-animalcule" is derived; a "foot" ending in two "toes" at the hind end; an alimentary canal running from a mouth at the front to an anus just above the base of the foot, with, just inside the mouth, a chamber with hard pieces inside it forming the "mastax"; a nervous system with a concentration at the front; an excretory system consisting of two tubes on either side originating in flame-cells and leading into the

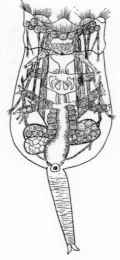

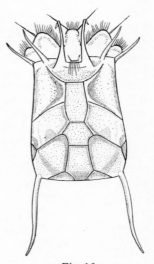

Fig. 15
Brachionus mülleri Ehrenb.
(after Wesenberg-Lund)

Fig. 16
Keratella quadrata Müller
(after Garnett)

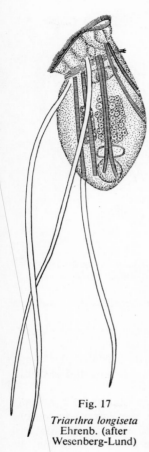

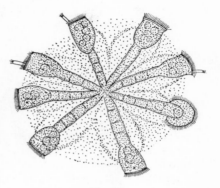

Fig. 18

Conochilus unicornis Rouss. (after
Wesenberg-Lund)

Fig. 17

Triarthra longiseta
Ehrenb. (after
Wesenberg-Lund)

end part of the gut; with a contractile bladder; with an ovary consisting of a germ sac and a yolk sac
also opening into the hind end of
the gut; and with muscles. No cir-
culatory or respiratory system (fig.
15).

Shape and form very variable
(figs. 15–20); cuticle either thin and
flexible or hard and divided into
plates (fig. 16), which may bear
spines. Many species inside a gelatinous capsule or occasionally a
thin hard tube. Some build a pro-
tective case from extraneous objects. *Conochilus* is
colonial (fig. 18). Males smaller than females and without
gut. They are found but rarely, and those of most species
have never been seen. Some free-swimming all their lives;
some sessile; some attached much of the time but capable

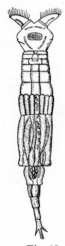

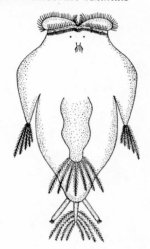

Fig. 19
Philodina roseola Ehrenb.
(after Garnett)

Fig. 20
Pedalion mirum Hudson
(after Wesenberg-Lund)

of swimming to another station; some parasitic in animals or plants.

The most characteristic features are the "wheel organ" and the mastax, but a few species lack cilia.

The foot may also be absent, particularly in planktonic forms (fig. 17). A few species have no anus and eject undigestible remains through the mouth.

The organism most likely to be mistaken for a rotifer is the planktonic larva of *Dreissena*, the Zebra Mussel, but it has its mouth at the side, not at the front, lacks foot and mastax, and has no reproductive organs. Some may be mistaken for ciliates until close microscopic examination reveals their more complex structure; the smallest rotifers are smaller than the largest ciliates . . Phylum **Rotifera**

200–300 spp.   Hudson, C. T., and Gosse, P. H. (1886 and supplement 1889), *The Rotifera or Wheel-animalcules*, 2 vols.

London: Longmans, Green.
Voigt, M. (1957), *Rotatoria.*
Die Rädertiere Mitteleuropas,
2 vols. Berlin: Bornträger.

— Without the above combination of characters . . 8

8. Very small organisms, none
more than 2 mm long. Body
generally elongate and forked
at the hind end. Cuticle
usually bearing spines and
scales. Cilia at the front end
and on parts of the upper and
lower surfaces; those at the
front end often long. Gut running from mouth at the front
end straight to an anus at the
hind end. Nervous and ex-
cretory system as in rotifers;
no mastax or bladder.

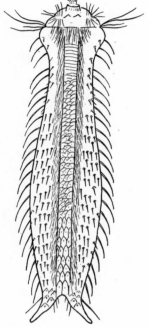

Fig. 21
Chaetonotus maximus Ehrenb.
(after Wesenberg-Lund)

Most of the time the animals
crawl, but they can swim by
means of the long cilia at the
front.

Most Gastrotricha are re-
cognizable immediately by
their shape and the spines and other excrescences.

Fig. 21. Collin, A. (1912), S.W.F.D. . Phylum **Gastrotricha**

— Without the above combination of characters . . 9

9. Very small organisms, with one (figs. 22 and 23) or two
(fig. 24) suckers. With (fig. 22) or without a tail, which may
be forked . . Cercaria stage of Class **Trematoda**

These are immature stages of members of a class in which all
the adults are parasitic, generally on vertebrates. There are
two main orders; the Monogena, which have but one host

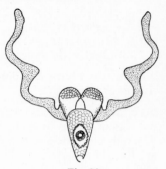

Fig. 23
Bucephalus polymorphus Baer.
(after Wesenberg-Lund)

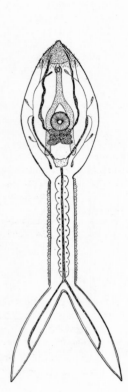

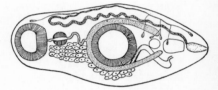

Fig. 24
Cercariaeum limnaeae auriculariae
(after Wesenberg-Lund)

Fig. 22
*Furcocercaria frederiks-
borgensis* Wesenberg-
Lund (after Wesenberg-
Lund)

Fig. 25
Portion of a polyzoan colony

and on which the adult stage is generally an external parasite, and the free-swimming larva seeks an animal of the same kind as the one its parent infested; and the Digena, which have a more complex life-history, with two or three hosts in which the adult is always an internal parasite, and two free-swimming stages, the miracidium and the cercaria. The miracidium, a small delicate cilia-covered organism, is apparently not captured by people making a general collection of freshwater organisms, but the cercaria sometimes is. The miracidium often attacks a snail, in which there is further development leading to the production of cercariae. These may bore directly into a vertebrate host, which is man in the case of the well-known *Schistosoma* (*Bilharzia*), encyst externally on some object which the vertebrate host is likely to eat as in the case of *Fasciola* (*Distomum*), which causes liver-rot in sheep, or encyst in the muscles of a fish in the case of species whose vertebrate host is a fish-eating bird.

Dawes, B. (1956), *The Trematoda*. Cambridge U.P.

Nasit, P. and Erasmus, D.A. (1964). A key to the cercariae from British freshwater molluscs. *J. Helminth.* **38**, 245–268.

Without the above combination of characters . . 10

10. Animals colonial, i.e. a number of heads (lophophores) are all connected to a common body, each head bearing a number of tentacles, which are ciliated (provided with minute lashing hairs). Colonies usually attached but sometimes able to creep very slowly. . . . Moss Animalcules or Pipe Moss Phylum **Polyzoa** (Bryozoa)

Fig. 25. About 12 spp.

— Not colonial 11

11. Animals with a hard inflexible shell (a soft body with no trace of segmentation projects from this shell when the animal is active)
Snails and Mussels Phylum MOLLUSCA, Key 2, p. 15

— Animals without a hard inflexible shell . . . 12

12. Segmented or unsegmented, generally worm-like animals usually with a soft integument that permits lateral expansion and contraction; if the integument is rigid, the animal is not segmented. Never with jointed limbs and rarely with appendages of any kind   .   .   "Worms" Key 3, p. 24

— Segmented animals covered with a hard, jointed integument so that the shape of the body cannot be altered or altered only a little; usually with limbs

Phylum ARTHROPODA Key 4, p. 33

These three large groups are immediately and easily separable, with one exception: larvae of some of the flies (Order Diptera, Class Insecta) lack legs and may have a superficially worm-like appearance. None, however, has more than 14 segments, and most worms have more than this or are unsegmented. The most worm-like are the Ceratopogonidae (fig. 158), for they are long relative to their diameter, and they swim by undulations of the body. Close examination, however, shows that they have a distinct head of the shape characteristic of the family. Some of the maggot-like larvae have no distinct head, but they commonly have more robust jaws than any worm, and often those characteristic insect organs— spiracles, the holes through which they breathe. The beginner who is still in doubt is advised to compare figs. 58–63 with figs. 148–175.

Key 2

MOLLUSCA

THERE are a number of handbooks to this popular group, e.g. Germain, L. (1930, 1931), F.F. 21 and 22; Ehrmann, P. (1933), T.M.E. 2; and, for snails only, Ellis, A. E. (1926), *British Snails*: Oxford.

1. Snails, i.e. with a single shell which is helically wound, coiled in one plane, or limpet-like . . GASTROPODA 2

    Macan, T. T. (1969), S.P.F.B.A. 13.

— Bivalves, i.e. with two valves or shells joined by a hinge
    LAMELLIBRANCHIATA 11

    Ellis, A. E. (1962), L.S.S.B.F. 13.

2. Operculates, i.e. snails with an operculum—that is, a horny or calcified plate which closes the mouth of the shell when

Fig. 26
Viviparus fasciatus (Müller)

the animal is retracted and which is carried on the back when the animal is expanded (fig. 26); respiration by means of gills 3

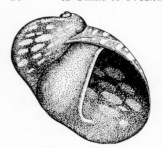

Fig. 27
Theodoxus fluviatilis
6 mm high

— Pulmonates, i.e. snails without an operculum; respiration by means of a lung, though a few have redeveloped a gill-like organ (much or all of the gaseous exchange may be through the body surface and the lung may be full of water) 8

3. Shell round with a small spire, resembling in its thick robustness a marine rather than a freshwater snail; aperture half-moon shaped; shell usually with a pattern of purple, pink or white variegations on a yellow, brown or black background . . . . . **Neritidae**

Fig. 27. *Theodoxus (Neritina) fluviatilis* (Linn.). Fairly common on stones in calcareous lakes and rivers.

— Shell with a taller spire, and thinner; aperture more or less round; shell pattern, if present, not variegated . . 4

4. Shell over 30 mm high; usually banded . . **Viviparidae**

Figs. 28 and 29. 2 spp. in *Viviparus*. In sluggish parts of calcareous rivers, canals, etc., in south and east England.

Fig. 28
Viviparus viviparus (Linn.)
35 mm high

Fig. 29
Viviparus fasciatus (Müller)
36 mm high

— Shell under 15 mm high; seldom banded .   .   . 5

5. Shell, if higher than broad, only just so; when the animal is expanded the thread-like right gill and feather-like left gill are protruded outside the shell .   .   **Valvatidae**

Figs. 30, 31 and 32. 3 spp. in *Valvata*.

Fig. 30	Fig. 31	Fig. 32
Valvata cristata	*Valvata macrostoma*	*Valvata piscinalis*
Müller 4 mm across	Steenbuch 2 mm high	(Müller) 5 mm high

— Shell distinctly higher than broad; the comb-like gills not visible when the animal is extended .   HYDROBIIDAE 6

6. Height at least 6 mm and up to 12 mm .   .   **Bithynia**

Figs. 33 and 34. 2 spp. found in calcareous water.

Fig. 33	Fig. 34
Bithynia tentaculata	*Bithynia leachii* (Sheppard)
(Linn.) 9·5 mm high	6·5 mm high

— Height less than 6 mm 7

7. Shell rather squat, with a characteristic blunt tip and about 4 whorls . . . . **Amnicola taylori** (Smith)

    Fig. 35. In canals near Manchester and in a dock at Grange-mouth in Stirling.

— Shell tall and pointed with about 5½ whorls
    Hydrobia (*Paludestrina* or *Potamopyrgus*) **jenkinsi** Smith

    Fig. 36. Widespread and often in great numbers.
    Note. Several other operculates are found in brackish water.

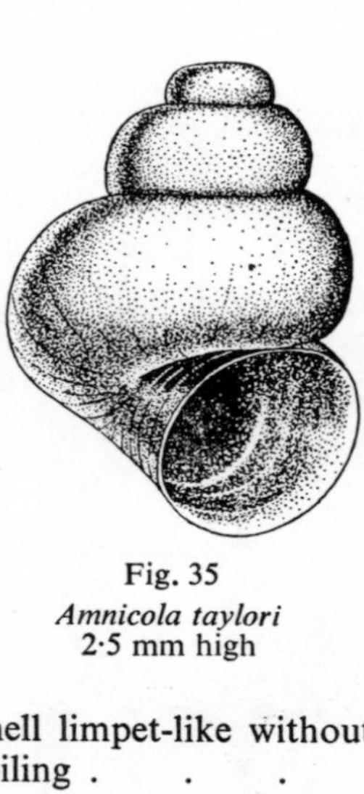

Fig. 35
Amnicola taylori
2·5 mm high

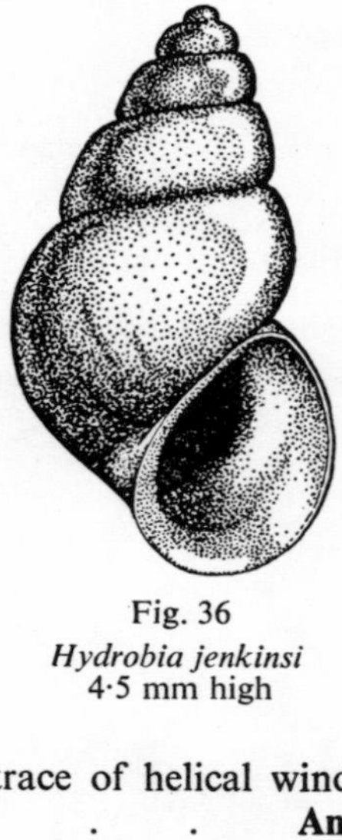

Fig. 36
Hydrobia jenkinsi
4·5 mm high

8. Shell limpet-like without any trace of helical winding or coiling . . . . **Ancylidae**

    Figs. 37 and 38. 2 spp., one (*A. fluviatile*) attached to bare rocks and stones, the other to stems and leaves of plants.

-- Not thus 9

9. Shell helically wound and taller than broad . . 10

Fig. 37
Ancylus lacustris (Linn.) 2 mm high

 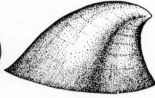

Fig. 38
Ancylastrum fluviatile (Müller) 5 mm high

— Shell coiled almost in one plane, and much broader than
tall . . . . . Ramshorns **Planorbidae**

Figs. 39–42. 13 spp. in *Planorbis* and 1 in *Segmentina*.

Fig. 39
Segmentina nitida (Müller)
6 mm across

Fig. 40
Planorbis complanatus
(Linn.) 5 mm across

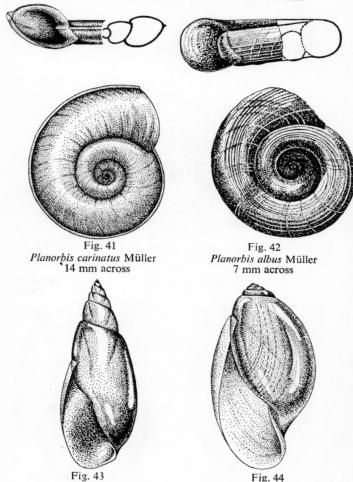

Fig. 41
Planorbis carinatus Müller
14 mm across

Fig. 42
Planorbis albus Müller
7 mm across

Fig. 43
Aplecta hypnorum 10 mm high

Fig. 44
Physa fontinalis 10 mm high

10. Shell sinistral, i.e. if it be held upright with the aperture towards the observer the aperture is to the observer's left;

shell thin; tentacles awl-shaped . . **Physidae**

> *Aplecta hypnorum* (Linn.) (fig. 43), *Physa fontinalis* (Linn.)
> (fig. 44) and two, possibly more, introduced species of *Physa*.

— Shell dextral and thicker; tentacles triangular

Limnaeidae

> Figs. 45–51. 6 spp. and 1 introduced sp. confined to Leith in
> *Limnaea*, 1 rare sp. in *Myxas*.

Fig. 45
Myxas glutinosa
(Müller) 14 mm high

Fig. 46
Limnaea pereger
(Müller) 11 mm high

Fig. 47
Limnaea auricularia
(Linn.) 20 mm high

Fig. 48
Limnaea stagnalis
(Linn.) 50 mm
high

Fig. 49
Limnaea trunca-
tula (Müller)
7 mm high

Fig. 50
Limnaea glabra
(Müller) 10 mm
high

Fig. 51
Limnaea palustris
(Müller) 22 mm
high

11. Shell large to medium-sized; almost triangular when seen end on; attached to the substratum by threads (byssus)
Dreissensiidae

Fig. 52. *Dreissena* (*Dreissensia*) *polymorpha* (Pallas), the Zebra Mussel. This fairly recently introduced species occurs in canals, reservoirs, etc., and sometimes inside pipes. It is the only freshwater mollusc with a free-swimming larva.

Fig. 52
Dreissena polymorpha 31 mm long

— Shell large or small; each half with smoothly curved outline when seen end on; not attached to the substratum, usually living almost completely buried in the mud . 12

12. Shell at least 25 mm long, usually more; edges of the mantle separate . . Freshwater Mussels **Unionidae**

Figs. 53 and 54. *Margaritifera* 2 spp., *Unio* 2 spp., *Anodonta* 3 spp.

Fig. 53
Margaritifera margaritifera (Linn.) 118 mm long

Fig. 54
Anodonta cygnaea (Linn.) 104 mm long

— Shell less than 25 mm long; edges of the mantle fused ventrally except for a slit through which the foot comes out
Pea Mussels SPHAERIIDAE 13

13. Shell more or less symmetrical on either side of the hinge. Two siphons . . . . . **Sphaerium**

Fig. 55. 4 spp.

Fig. 55
Sphaerium corneum (Linn.) 5 mm long

— Shell not symmetrical. One siphon. .   .   **Pisidium**
  Fig. 56.   15 spp.

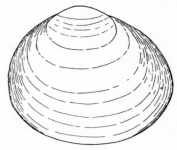

Fig. 56
Pisidium lilljeborgii Clessin 3·5 mm long

Key 3

"WORMS"

1. Unsegmented. Without bristles or suckers.   .   . 2

— Body divided by constrictions into a usually large number
  of segments. Either with bristles on the segments or a
  sucker usually at both front and hind end. (The bundles of
  bristles at intervals along the body are sometimes the best
  indication of the segmentation. In the larger earthworm-
  like representatives the bristles are short setae deeply
  embedded in the body and much less conspicuous than
  those of the smaller, generally more transparent, worms) 7

2. Round and elongate. Body enclosed in a rigid cuticle
  which prevents lateral contraction and expansion. No
  cilia. Swimming by undulating movements of the body
                    Phylum NEMATODA, etc. 5

— Variable in shape, often flat, never very elongate. Body not enclosed in a rigid cuticle and capable of lateral contraction and expansion. Cilia present. Swimmers swim by means of the cilia. (Excretion by means of cells with a flagellum inside, the beating of which resembles the flickering of a candle flame, whence the name "flame cell"; each flame cell leads into a duct and the ducts from the various cells join)   3

3. A small reddish-yellow worm about 1 cm long. Above the mouth there is a protrusible proboscis armed with a tooth at the end. Gut open at both ends   Class **Nemertini**

> *Prostoma graecense* Böhmig may be the only representative of this predominantly marine and terrestrial group; it lives in a tube in running water and is perhaps commoner than generally thought.

— If a proboscis is present, the gut opens at the end of it. Only one opening to the gut
            Class TURBELLARIA (Phylum PLATYHELMINTHES) 4

> One of the diagnostic features of this phylum is the absence of a true body-cavity and blood system, but this is not of much value as an aid to recognition by the field-worker. Many Turbellaria progress by means of cilia with a steady glide like that of a snail, and this is a distinctive feature of living specimens. Some of the smaller ones swim and resemble ciliate Protozoa, but are more complex internally.

4. Gut with three branches, one pointing forwards, two pointing backwards, opening at the end of a proboscis in the middle of the body. More than 6 mm long. Movement a steady glide over the substratum. Always flat; colour brown, black, yellow or whitish, never conspicuous
            Flatworms Order **Tricladida**

> Fig. 57.   13 spp.   Common on the bottom of streams, lake-shores and ponds. Reynoldson, T. B. (1967), F.B.A.S.P. 23.

Fig. 57
Polycelis nigra (Ehrenb.) 8 mm long

— Gut a simple tube, which may have side pouches; opening
near the front end of the body. Most under 2 mm long.
Movement a steady glide over the substratum, but the
smallest can swim. Shape various; often bright green or
yellow or red. (May reproduce by budding, and columns of
three or four individuals not yet separated are common)

Order **Rhabdocoelida**

Probably about 200 spp.   Steinmann, P., and Bresslau,
E. (1913), *Die Strudelwürmer*. Leipzig: Klinkhardt.

5. Less than 10 mm long, some less than 1 mm long
Roundworms **Nematoda**

Many different kinds of nematode are to be found in debris
from the bottom of ponds and sluggish streams and in
vegetation; they are also numerous in the soil. Many are
parasitic and some of these have a free-living aquatic stage.
It is probable that a great number of species have yet to be
described.

Fig. 58.   Goodey, T. and J. B. (1963),   *Soil and freshwater nematodes*.

Fig. 58
A nematode schematic (after Schneider)

— Length 40–190 mm, one species ranging up to 560 mm . 6

6. Anterior end pointed; body tapering; cuticle finely striated and somewhat transparent . . Rainworms **Mermithidae**

— Anterior end blunt; body cylindrical; cuticle rough and beset with fine papillae . Horsehair Worms **Gordiacea**

Heinze, K. (1941), T.W.D. 39.

These striking animals, of which the main feature is summed up in the name "Horsehair Worm", are parasitic in the larval stage in various animals, some of which are terrestrial. Most of the Mermithidae are terrestrial and may appear after rain—whence the name. Though superficially the two groups are similar, internally there are marked differences and the Gordiacea are usually not considered as belonging to the Nematoda, though near this group.

7. With a sucker at both ends; never with bristles
Leeches Class **Hirudinea**

13 spp. Mann, K. H. (1965), F.B.A.S.P. 14

— Never with a sucker at both ends, one small family, found attached to crayfishes, with a sucker at the hind end; except for this last, all with bristles grouped into bundles of which there are one on either side towards the ventral line and generally one more on either side near the dorsal line; in a few species only one bristle per bundle
True Worms Class OLIGOCHAETA 8

Brinkhurst, R. O. (1963), F.B.A.S.P. 22. Ude, H. (1929), T.W.D.15.

8. No bristles. A sucker at the hind end. Small (at most 12 mm long), relatively broad worms living attached to crayfish . . **Branchiobdellidae** (Discodrilidae)

Fig. 59. Probably not more than 2 or 3 spp.

— Bristles present. No suckers. Free-living . . . 9

9. Reproduction generally asexual, each worm consisting of a chain of two or more parts that will ultimately split off to become individuals. (Most are small rather transparent worms with numerous long bristles) . . . 10

— Reproduction usually sexual, sometimes by the splitting of an individual into several pieces, but never by chain formation 22

10. Numerous long hair-like bristles in dórsal and ventral bundles. Integument of most species with globules coloured red, yellow, or green. No internal walls between the segments of the body. (Small transparent worms not more

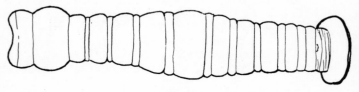

Fig. 59
Branchiobdella parasita Henle 10 mm long (after Ude)

than 10 mm long. A patch in front of the mouth with cilia, which are used for swimming) . . . **Aelosomatidae**

About 5 spp. all in the genus *Aelosoma*.

— Never with hair-like bristles in both dorsal and ventral bundles. Integument without coloured globules. Walls between each segment . . . . NAIDIDAE 11

These small worms live among plants in contrast to most of the rest which live in mud. Some are free-swimming, some inhabit tubes. They show the greatest adaptation to aquatic existence. The genera are diverse and it is easier to key them out individually than to compile a composite diagnosis of the whole family.

11. Bristles confined to under surface of body; wanting on segments 3, 4 and 5; the worm walks on these bristles and sometimes loops like a caterpillar. Front end oblique in side view. Traces of testes and ovaries in segments 5 and 6. Up to 15 mm long . . . . . **Chaetogaster**

    Fig. 60.   About 6 spp.

— Without the above combination of characters . . 12

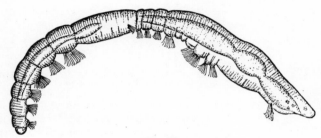

Fig. 60
Chaetogaster limnaei v. Baer, 2 mm long (after Wesenberg-Lund)

12. Without hair-like bristles in the dorsal bundles . . 13

— With hair-like bristles in the dorsal bundles . . 15

13. Third segment much longer than fourth. Third segment and all behind it with dorsal bundles of bristles. 1–1·5 mm long . . . . **Amphichaeta leydigi** Tauber

— Third segment not longer than fourth. Second, fifth or sixth segment and all behind with dorsal bundles of bristles 14

14. Forked curved bristles (fig. 61) in dorsal and ventral bundles. 5–18 mm long . . . . **Paranais**
    2 spp.

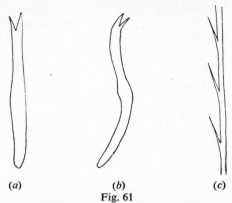

(*a*)   (*b*)   (*c*)
Fig. 61

(*a*) A forked straight bristle. (*b*) A forked curved bristle. (*c*) A frayed
bristle of *Vejdovskyella* (after Ude)

— Forked curved bristles in the ventral bundles, forked
   straight bristles (fig. 61) in the dorsal bundles. 7–36 mm
   long   .   .   .   **Ophidonais serpentina** (Müller)

15. Dorsal bundles on segments 2 and all behind. 2–6 mm long
    Pristina longiseta Ehrenberg

It is likely that some of the other European species occur in
Britain too.

Fig. 62

Hind end of *Dero per-
rieri* Bousfield from
above (after Ude)

— No dorsal bundles on segments 2
   and 3 16

16. Gills at the hind end (retracted in
    preserved specimens)   .   . 17

— No gills   18

17. With two long slender gills and
    four shorter broader ones. 6–12 mm
    long . **Aulpohorus furcatus** (Oken)

— With no long slender gills (fig. 62).
   5–17 mm long   .   .   . **Dero**
        2 spp.

18. Bristles finely frayed (fig. 61). 3·5–8 mm long
Vejdovskyella comata (Vejdovsky)

— Bristles smooth 19

19. With a proboscis 20

— Without a proboscis 21

20. Dorsal bristles on segments 6, 7 and 8 very long. No ventral bundles present on segments 4 and 5. Length 2–7·5 mm (fig. 63) . . . **Ripistes parasita** (Schmidt)

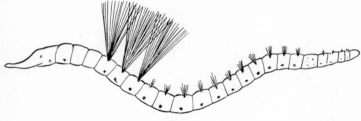

Fig. 63
Ripistes parasita (after Wesenberg-Lund) (5 mm long)*

— All dorsal bristles of same length. Ventral bundles present on segments 4 and 5. Up to 18 mm long . . **Stylaria**
2 spp.

21. Dorsal bristles on segment 6 very long, several times longer than the diameter of the body. 2–20 mm long
Slavina appendiculata (Udekem)

— Length of dorsal bristles nowhere more than twice the diameter of the body. 1–12 mm long . . **Nais**
About 5 spp.

* The original artist did not indicate the size of his specimen and this measurement has been obtained from another source. All such are enclosed in brackets.

22. Usually more than two bristles in at least some of the bundles   23

— Rarely more than two bristles to any of the bundles   . 24

23. Small, rather maggot-like worms up to 36 mm long; whitish, yellowish or reddish. Bristles straight or S-shaped, generally pointed. Spermathecae generally in segment 5, testes in segment 11, ovaries in segment 12 **Enchytraeidae**

    Most of the species in this large family are terrestrial.

— Small to large worms, up to 200 mm long. Some of the bristles forked at the tip. Spermathecal ducts opening on segment 10, testes in segment 10, ovaries in segment 11
Tubificidae

    About 20 spp.

24. Male openings on segment 12 or farther forward, inconspicuous or at the end of small tubes on the clitellum (this is the swelling which, on the earthworm, is popularly but erroneously believed to be the site of a join)   .   . 25

— Male openings generally on segment 15 but sometimes as far forward as segment 11; with conspicuous lips; clitellum beginning on segment behind the male openings   . 26

25. Small to medium-sized worms, 20–140 mm long; thicker than Tubificidae. Up to 8 bristles per segment in 2 ventral and 2 dorsal pairs; all pointed or forked at the tip; dorsal and ventral bristles generally similar. One or two pairs of testes in the region of segments 8, 9 and 10, one or two pairs of ovaries generally in the segments behind them, one to five pairs of spermathecae before or behind the testes and ovaries .   .   .   .   . **Lumbriculidae**

    About 12 spp.

— Very long thin worms up to 300 mm in length. Bristles single, 4 or 2 per segment, there being sometimes no dorsal ones; dorsal bristles larger than the ventral ones, pointed and curved at the tip. Two pairs of testes in segments 10 and 11, two pairs of ovaries in segments 12 and 13, three pairs of spermathecae in front of the testes

Phreoryctidae (Haplotaxidae)

2 spp.

26. First segment produced into a slight cone without any lobes. Bristles in pairs. Clitellum not always visible in mature worms . . . . . **Criodrilidae**

The single species in this family, though widespread in Europe, has not been recorded in Britain.

— First segment divided into a projecting median lobe and, on the underside, into two lateral lobes. Bristles in pairs or single. Clitellum always visible in mature worms. Small, medium-sized or large earthworm-like worms

Lumbricidae

About 10 spp., most occurring in terrestrial as well as aquatic biotopes.

Gerard, B. M. (1963), L.S.S.B.F. 6.

Key 4

ARTHROPODA

THIS phylum is characterized by a hard external skeleton, like a suit of armour, and jointed limbs which are absent only in some young and some parasitic forms. It includes a great variety of freshwater animals, some small but some bigger than any other invertebrate. It is divided into three groups called classes by some authors and sub-phyla by others:

Arachnida: Water-mites and the water-spider.

Crustacea: Crayfish, shrimps, hoglice, water-fleas and others.

Insecta: Insects.

The Crustacea are divided into four classes, subclasses or orders: Phyllopoda (fairy shrimps, apus, and water-fleas), Copepoda (*Cyclops*), Ostracoda and Malacostraca (higher crustaceans such as crayfish, shrimps and hoglice).

The young of Malacostraca and all water-fleas (Order Cladocera) except *Leptodora* are carried by their mothers, and when set free are miniature versions of the adults. The rest are set free in a nauplius stage which passes through a metanauplius stage before reaching adulthood.

1. Small animals with globular or pear-shaped bodies and three (nauplii) or four (metanauplii) pairs of limbs; limbs with hairs or bristles and some of them generally branched (figs. 64 and 65). The young stages of ostracods have two valves or shells like the adults

   Immature Crustacea (see above)

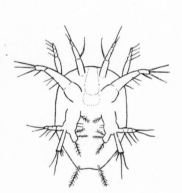

Fig. 64
Nauplius of *Cyclops*
(0·3 mm long)
(after Wesenberg-Lund)

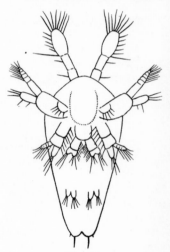

Fig. 65
Metanauplius of *Diaptomus*
(0·4 mm long) (after
Wesenberg-Lund)

— Without the above combination of characters . . 2

2. With 8 legs in the adult and 6 in the immature stage. Body more or less globular, the greatest part of it un-

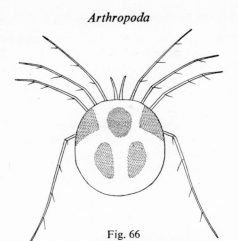

Fig. 66
A water-mite of the Hydrachnellae 1·5 mm long

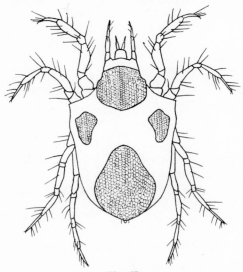

Fig. 67
A water-mite of the Halacaridae 0·5 mm long

segmented (figs. 66 and 67). Or with stumpy legs and a shape vaguely suggesting a bear (fig. 68)

Class ARACHNIDA, Key 4a, p. 36

— Not thus 3

3. With 6 legs or without legs. Body consisting of a head bearing the mouthparts, one pair of antennae (feelers), and other sense organs; a thorax bearing the legs; and an abdomen of usually about 9 visible segments without appendages except cerci at the hind end. But some of the fly larvae (figs. 145–175) lack legs and often a distinct head, and have a somewhat worm-like appearance (see above, p. 14) . . . . Class INSECTA, Key 4c, p. 49

— Usually more than 6 legs. Segmentation of the body and position and structure of the appendages variable, but never as in the two preceding classes. Never legless and worm-like . . Class CRUSTACEA, Key 4b, p. 38

Key 4a

ARACHNIDA

IT is simpler not to use a key for this group, since only three categories are distinguished. First is the water-spider, *Argyroneta aquatica* Cl., which looks like any medium-sized spider, but which is the only member of its group to have adopted a truly aquatic mode of life.

Second come the water-mites, commonly known as the Hydracarina, though not all authors use that name today. There are some 250 British species, arranged in families in different ways by different authors. Probably naturalists will either get really interested in this group or remain content to list specimens of it simply as "water-mites", and accordingly it is proposed here to notice only the two major divisions recognized by Viets (1936):

1. Legs radiating. Palp 5-segmented with the second segment not elongated. Adults swim or crawl. Larvae, as far as is known, usually parasitic. (fig. 66) . . **Hydrachnellae**

2. First two pairs of legs directed forwards, last two backwards. Palp with at most four segments, the second elongate. Adults crawl. Larvae free-swimming. (fig. 67)
Halacaridae

Most Halacaridae are marine, but there are a few freshwater species all small, less than 1 mm long. The Hydrachnellae are mainly freshwater, though a few are marine, and generally somewhat larger.

Mites of the first group are small globular creatures either bright red or conspicuously patterned in blue or green and brown or yellow. Many swim, but those that live in streams only crawl. The larvae, which have but three legs, are familiar objects attached to water-bugs and other insects. Some are found on aerial insects, others on bivalve molluscs.

Soar, C. D., and Williamson, W. (1925, 27, 29), R.S. 3 vols.
Viets, K. (1936), T.W.D. 31 and 32.

Thirdly come the bear animalcules or Tardigrada, which are often included with the Arachnids because they have four pairs of legs, though their real affinities are probably elsewhere and almost certainly remote from any known group. They are very small—less than 1 mm long—somewhat grub-like creatures with stumpy legs at intervals down the body. Most dwell in damp soil or moss, but a few are true freshwater animals. The specimen illustrated in fig. 68 is actually a marine species.

Marcus, E. (1928), T.W.D. 12.

Fig. 68
Echiniscoides sigismundi (Schultze) 0·2 mm long (after Marcus)

Key 4b

CRUSTACEA

1. With at least ten consecutive similar appendages which are leaf-like and which, moving one after the other from the front backwards, drive the animal along

   Subclass PHYLLOPODA or Branchiopoda

   Order EUPHYLLOPODA 2

   Borradaile, Potts, Eastham and Saunders (1932), in *The Invertebrata*. Cambridge U.P. rate this a class; Wesenberg-Lund calls it an order. I have compromised.

— Never with as many as 10 consecutive limbs similar . 3

2. Without a carapace (a shield-like plate covering the top of the forepart of the body). Swims back downwards

   The Fairy Shrimp **Cheirocephalus diaphanus** Prévost

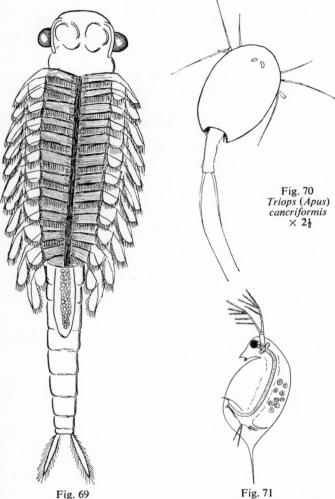

Fig. 70
*Triops (Apus)
cancriformis*
× 2½

Fig. 69
Cheirocephalus diaphanus 22 mm
long (from p.s.)

Fig. 71
Daphnia pulex (De Geer) 3 mm
long (after Wesenberg-Lund)

Fig. 69.   These creatures, about 25 mm long, are sometimes to be found swimming in temporary pools.

— With a carapace; swims back upwards

Triops (*Apus*) **cancriformis** (Bosc)

Fig. 70.   This species, usually rather more than 25 mm long, is found in the same sort of places as *Cheirocephalus* but less frequently.

3. Usually larger Crustacea having the following limbs: two pairs of antennae, one pair of mandibles, and two pairs of maxillae to the head; 8 legs to the thorax, the first 3 sometimes modified as mouthparts; 6 appendages, usually "swimmerets", to the abdomen, the last sometimes modified to form part of the tail fan

Subclass MALACOSTRACA 12

Hynes, H. B. N., Macan, T. T. and Williams, W. D. (1960), F.B.A.S.P. 19.

— Smaller Crustacea with fewer limbs 4

4. Body enclosed by a carapace having the form of two valves open along the ventral and hinged along the dorsal surface; all the limbs can be withdrawn within the valves, and many of the animals then have the appearance of a plant seed

Subclass **Ostracoda**

About 80 spp.   Klie, W. (1938), T.W.D. 34.

— If a carapace having the form of two valves is present, it does not enclose the head, and the antennae at least cannot be withdrawn within it 5

5. Body generally flat from side to side and enclosed by a carapace in the form of two valves (fig. 71). Three carnivorous genera of distinctive form have almost lost the carapace (figs. 73–75). Locomotion by means of the second antennae, which are two-branched. Body generally with no traces of segmentation apart from a series of limbs

Subclass PHYLLOPODA Order CLADOCERA 6

90 spp. in 8 families. In ponds and small pieces of water and free-swimming in lakes.

Scourfield, D. J., and Harding, J. P. (1958), F.B.A.S.P. 5.

— Body either pear-shaped (fig. 72), or with a flat shield-like carapace (fig. 77). Second antenna small and never used for locomotion. Except in *Argulus* (fig. 77), body obviously segmented . . .

Subclass COPEPODA 9

Gurney, R. (1931–1933), R.S. 3 vols.

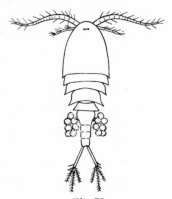

Fig. 72

Cyclops strenuus Fischer (1·5 mm long) (after Wesenberg-Lund)

6. Body enclosed by a carapace having the form of two valves, separate along the ventral edge; within the carapace five or six pairs of leaf-like appendages move to and fro and keep up a feeding current; dorsally the carapace encloses a brood-pouch. Fig. 71.

Water-fleas Sub-order **Calyptomera**

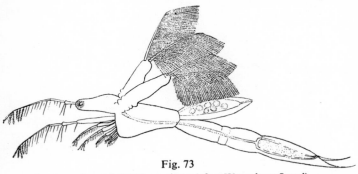

Fig. 73

Leptodora kindti 10 mm long (after Wesenberg-Lund)

— Carapace reduced and enclosing only a dorsal brood-pouch; carnivorous species with large second antennae and rather small limbs, which are not leaf-like

Sub-order GYMNOMERA 7

7. Four pairs of legs. Body compact . POLYPHEMIDAE 8

— Six pairs of legs. Body elongate

`LEPTODORIDAE **Leptodora kindti** (Focke)

Fig. 73.   A large (up to 10 mm long) animal found in the open water of lakes and large reservoirs.

8. Projection from hind end of body about as long as the body . . . . **Polyphemus pediculus** (Linn.)

Fig. 74.   Usually near the edges of lakes and in smaller bodies of water.

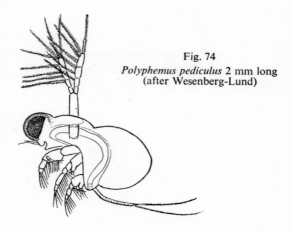

Fig. 74
Polyphemus pediculus 2 mm long
(after Wesenberg-Lund)

— Projection from hind end of body much longer than body
Bythotrephes

Fig. 75.   2 spp.   Free-swimming in lakes.

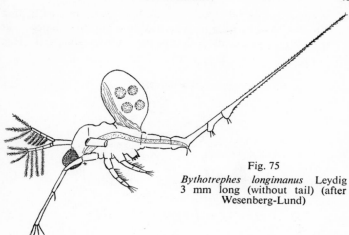

Fig. 75
Bythotrephes longimanus Leydig
3 mm long (without tail) (after
Wesenberg-Lund)

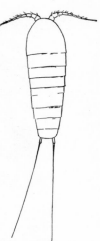

9. With a flat shield-like carapace, two
suckers and four pairs of swimming
limbs towards the hind end
Order BRANCHIURA **Argulus foliaceus**
Linn. A. coregoni Thorell

> Fig. 77. A parasite on fish which,
> however, can swim well and which is
> not uncommonly taken in plankton
> nets.

— Body pear-shaped or elongate with
no carapace and no suckers; swimming forms swim by means of the
long first antennae . . . 10

10. Fused head and thorax of same
width as abdomen and not clearly
separated from it. First antennae
very short, with never more than
10 segments. (Second antenna two-

Fig. 76
*Canthocamptus sta-
phylinus* (Jurine) just
under 1 mm long

branched. Egg-sac single.) Length of body not exceeding 1 mm. Crawling on aquatic plants and among the debris at the bottom of ponds and streams ` Order **Harpacticoidea**

Fig. 76. About 46 spp.

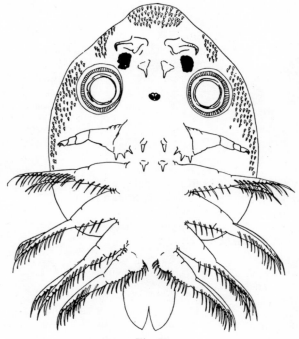

Fig. 77
Argulus foliaceus 6 mm long

— Fused head and thorax wider than abdomen and clearly separated from it. First antenna longer. Length generally about 2 mm. Free-swimming 11

11. First antenna with 22 to 25 segments (only 17 to 18 in the brackish-water genus *Acartia*). Second antenna

two-branched. Egg-sac single . . Order **Calanoidea**

14 spp., 6 in genus *Diaptomus*.

— First antenna with 6 to 17 segments. Second antenna unbranched. Egg-sac paired . . Order **Cyclopoidea**

Fig. 72. 37 free-living spp., most in genus *Cyclops*, which is sometimes split up. Harding, J. P. and Smith, W. A. (1960), F.B.A.S.P. 18 (both orders).

12. Without a carapace, i.e. the segments of the thorax are apparent when viewed from above (figs. 78–80). Eyes (when present) not on stalks 13

— With a carapace (figs. 81–83). Eyes on stalks . . 15

13. Very small (about 1 mm long) and rather elongate. Eight pairs of thoracic legs, each two-branched, except the last **Bathynella natans** Vejdovsky (*chappuisi* Delachaux)

Fig. 78. An inhabitant of subterranean waters occasionally found in wells.

— Larger and not elongate. Thoracic legs unbranched . 14

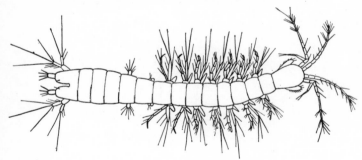

Fig. 78
Bathynella natans 1 mm long (after Thienemann)

14. Body like that of a woodlouse or slater, flattened from top to bottom. Second antennae at least three times as long as first antennae. Seven pairs of walking legs, the first thoracic limb being modified as a mouthpart. Abdominal limbs

two-branched, flat and leaf-like, constantly in motion, for they serve as gills. Eggs carried on the front part of the thorax underneath

Order ISOPODA The Water-hoglouse **Asellus**

Fig. 79. 3 spp. Ponds and lakes; abundant in waters recovering from sewage pollution. Walking is the method of locomotion.

Moon, H. P. (1953), *Proc. zool. Soc. Lond.* **123**, 411–417.

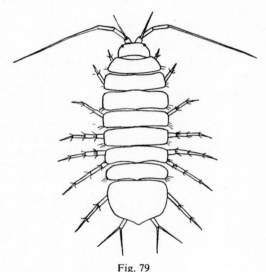

Fig. 79
An isopod, *Asellus* sp. 8 mm long

— Body like that of a sandhopper, flattened from side to side. Second antennae generally shorter than first antennae. First thoracic limb part of the mouthparts, 2nd and 3rd modified for grasping, 4th–8th simple. Abdominal appendages not flattened, 1st three pairs and 2nd three pairs dissimilar. Eggs carried between the bases of the thoracic limbs . . . . . . Order **Amphipoda**

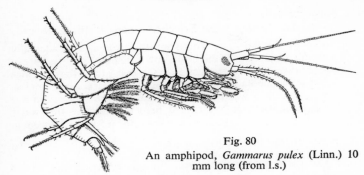

Fig. 80
An amphipod, *Gammarus pulex* (Linn.) 10
mm long (from l.s.)

Gammarus 4 spp. (fig. 80); *Crangonyx gracilis* Smith;
Orchestia bottae Edwards; *Niphargus* 4 spp. *Gammarus* swims
quite well and also crawls. It frequently progresses on its side
and seeks shelter beneath stones and other objects. *Crangonyx*
is similar, but its habit of crawling about upright distinguishes
a living population at once. *Orchestia* can swim, but is
generally found just out of the water beneath stones; it jumps
like its relative, the sandhopper, if the stone is lifted up.
Niphargus occurs in caves, wells and occasionally springs.

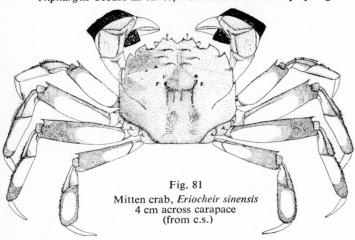

Fig. 81
Mitten crab, *Eriocheir sinensis*
4 cm across carapace
(from c.s.)

15. Body crab-like

The Mitten Crab **Eriocheir sinensis** Milne-Edwards

Fig. 81. Not British. This species, introduced accidentally from China towards the beginning of the century, has spread from the point of introduction in Germany to all the countries bordering the Baltic Sea and down all the west coast of France. One specimen was taken in Britain, but the species did not establish itself. It is included here in case any freshwater biologist wants to keep an eye open for a further invasion.

— Body shrimp-like or lobster-like   16

16. Body shrimp-like. Carapace, though covering the whole thorax, fused only with the first three segments. First thoracic limb one of the mouthparts, rest two-branched. Abdominal limbs reduced; eggs carried at base of thoracic limbs   .   .   Order MYSIDACEA **Mysis relicta** Lovén

Fig. 82. In the open water of Ennerdale (Cumberland), Lough Neagh (N. Ireland) and a few other big lakes. *Neomysis integer* (Leach) (*vulgaris* Thompson) is a brackish-water species which, however, is often found in ponds reached so rarely by the sea that the water is quite fresh most of the time. Several shrimp-like species, belonging, however, to the Decapoda, occur in brackish water.

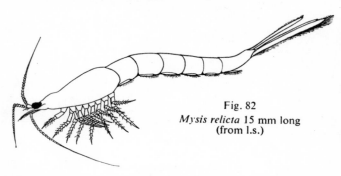

Fig. 82
Mysis relicta 15 mm long
(from l.s.)

— Body lobster-like. Carapace fused with all the thoracic segments. First three thoracic limbs modified as mouth-

parts, 4th modified into large "pincers", rest walking legs. Abdominal limbs not reduced, and in the female used for carrying eggs . . . Order DECAPODA Crayfish
Astacus (*Potamob:us*) **pallipes** Lereboullet

Fig. 83. In streams, rivers and lakes, but absent from soft waters. *Astacus astacus* Linn. (*fluviatilis* Fabricius) has been introduced several times, but has never established itself permanently as far as is known.

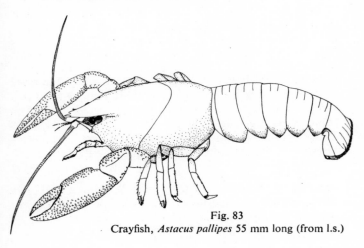

Fig. 83
Crayfish, *Astacus pallipes* 55 mm long (from l.s.)

Key 4c

INSECTA

1. With hard wing-covers and usually a pair of membranous wings beneath (a difficulty arises here because in a few bugs wings or wing-covers are incomplete or absent, but it is generally possible to tell from the size whether a specimen taken at a season when both are about is an adult or a

nymph; if not, the genitalia must be examined) (figs. 177–201) . . . Adults of the Orders Hemiptera (bugs) and Coleoptera (beetles) Key 4c, pt. 4, p. 98

— Wings and wing-covers absent or extending only to the second or third abdominal segment . . . Adult Collembola (springtails) and nymphs and larvae of the remaining Orders 2

2. With short wings or wing-pads extending to the second or third abdominal segment (these, however, do not appear until the nymphs are at least half-grown). With either two (figs. 86–88) long tapering tails at the hind end of the body, or with three (figs. 90–107) such tails, or with a beak (figs. 190, 191, 192, 196, 197; it is folded under the body in the other species) or characteristic triangular head (fig. 176), or with a "mask" that can be projected forward in front of the head (fig. 112) . . . Nymphs of Plecoptera (stoneflies), Ephemeroptera (mayflies), Hemiptera (bugs) and Odonata (dragon-flies)

Key 4c, pt. 1. p. 51

— With no trace of wings or wing pads. Without a beak, two or three long tapering tails (short ones are present in the dytiscid beetle larvae (figs. 135, 136)), or a mask . . 3

3. With three pairs of jointed thoracic legs . . Adult Collembola (springtails) and larvae of Neuroptera and Megaloptera (alder-flies, etc.), Trichoptera (caddis-flies), Lepidoptera (moths) and most Coleoptera (beetles)

Key 4c, pt. 2, p. 64

— Never with jointed legs, usually without any legs at all Larvae of Diptera (flies) and a few Coleoptera (beetles)

Key 4c, pt. 3, p. 83

Key 4c, pt. 1

1. Mouthparts in the form of a beak (figs. 190, 196), or head of a characteristic triangular shape (fig. 176)

     HEMIPTERA (bugs) 2

— Mouthparts of typical biting type or lowermost piece (labium) modified into a hinged mask that can be shot forward to catch prey (fig. 112) 3

2. The hind legs, being long, flat, and fringed with hairs, are efficient swimming organs; or with walking legs and breathing-tubes opening at the tip of a projection at the hind end (this is very short in small specimens)

     Nymphal Hemiptera, submerged forms

    These resemble adults (p. 109) in general form, but cannot be identified to species.

— Hind legs not modified for swimming; breathing-tubes not opening at the tip of a terminal projection. Dwelling on the water surface . . **Nymphal Hemiptera,** surface forms

    These resemble adults (p. 105) in general form, but cannot be identified to species.

3. With two long tapering cerci or "tails". Gills, when present, on the underside of the thorax. (Crawling nymphs)

     Stoneflies Order PLECOPTERA 4

    Figs. 84–89.   Hynes, H. B. N. (1967), F.B.A.S.P. 17.

— With two long tapering cerci and a similar dorsal caudal appendage, making three "tails" in all. Gills along the side or the top of the abdomen, never on the thorax. Or with three broad plates at the end of the abdomen, or abdomen ending in three triangular points 8

4. Inner lobes of labium (glossae) distinctly smaller than outer (paraglossae) (fig. 84). Labrum more than twice as wide as long (fig. 84). Sternum (lower plate) on 10th

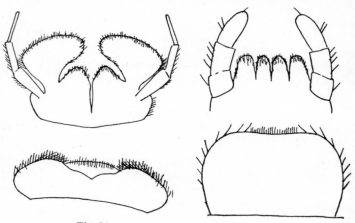

Fig. 84
Labium and labrum of perlid

Fig. 85
Labium and labrum of leuctrid

abdominal segment well developed. (Large- and medium-sized nymphs   .   **Perlodidae, Perlidae, Chloroperlidae**

Fig. 86.   10 spp. in 6 genera. The first two families contain the large species. The chloroperlids are smaller and resemble leuctrids. Their maxillary palp, with its very narrow last segment, is characteristic.

— Glossae and paraglossae of about same size (fig. 85). Labrum less than twice as wide as long (fig. 85). Tenth abdominal sternum reduced to a narrow lightly chitinized strip. (Small and medium-sized nymphs)   .   .   . 5

5. Each segment of the tarsus longer than the preceding. (Wing-pads oblique relative to the body; cf. fig. 87. Small or medium-sized nymphs living in fast or slow streams and rivers)   .   .   .   .   .   .   **Taeniopterygidae**

Possibly 4 spp. in 3 genera.

— Second segment of the tarsus shorter than the first   .   6

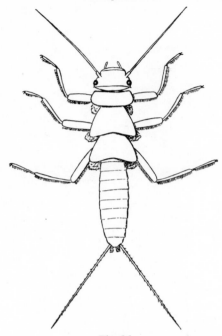

Fig. 86
Dinocras (Perla) cephalotes Klapalek (25 mm long) (from l.s.)

6. Cylindrical nymphs with the wing-pads parallel with the body. Elongate, the hind leg not reaching the tip of the abdomen when stretched back alongside it (fig. 88) . 7

— Stout nymphs with the wing-pads at an angle to the body. Short, the hind leg extending well beyond the tip of the abdomen when stretched back alongside it. (Small nymphs. The family includes the only members of the Order to be found in quiet water with mud and rooted plants)

Nemouridae

Fig. 87. 10 spp. in 4 genera.

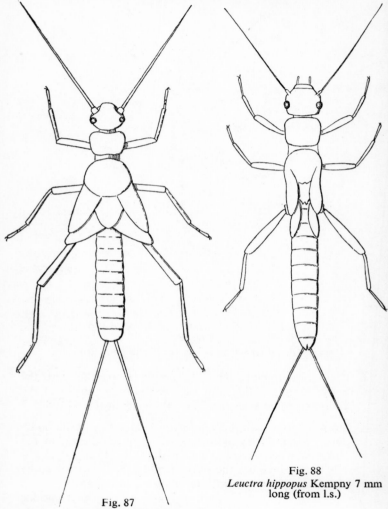

Fig. 88
Leuctra hippopus Kempny 7 mm
long (from l.s.)

Fig. 87
Nemurella inconspicua (Pictet) 8 mm long (from l.s.)

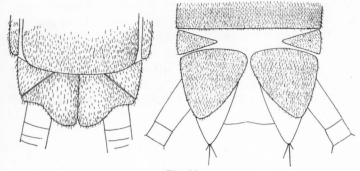

Fig. 89
Tip of abdomen from beneath of capniid (left) and leuctrid (right)

7. Abdominal segments 1–9 with chitinous plates above (terga) and below (sterna) and a narrow gap between them along the undersides (fig. 89, left). Sub-anal plates wider than long (fig. 89, left). (Small nymphs occurring in stony rivers) . . . . **Capniidae**

    3 spp. in genus *Capnia*.

— Abdominal segments 1–4 only with a separate tergum and sternum, rest encircled by a continuous chitinous ring. Sub-anal plates longer than wide (fig. 89, right). (Small nymphs found in stony places) . . **Leuctridae**

    Fig. 88. 6 spp. in genus *Leuctra*.

8. Three tails at the end of the abdomen. Mouthparts of biting type with no modifications

    Mayflies Order EPHEMEROPTERA 9

    Macan, T. T. (1970), F.B.A.S.P. 20.

— Three plates flat or triangular in cross-section (fig. 112), or three triangular points at the end of abdomen (fig. 113). Mouthparts of biting type, but the labium is modified and hinged in such a way that it can be projected in front of the head to seize prey (fig. 112)

    Dragon-flies Order ODONATA 16

    Gardner, A. E. (1954), *Ent. Gaz.* **5,** 157–171 and 193–213.

9. Gills beset with a close row of fine filaments down the sides, either held over the back (fig. 90), stretched out sideways (fig. 91), or concealed beneath a cover, which is in fact the second gill (fig. 92) 10

— Gills consisting of one plate (figs. 101, 102, 105 and 107), two plates (figs. 96 and 103), one plate and a tuft of filaments (fig. 93), or up to twelve filaments (figs. 97 and 98) 12

Fig. 90
Ephemera danica
Müller 24 mm long
(from l.s.)

Fig. 91
Potamanthus luteus
17 mm long

Fig. 92
Caenis sp. 5 mm long
(from l.s.)

10. Gills held over the back in life. Mandibles projecting in front of the head. Large nymphs burrowing in sand and mud . . . . **Ephemeridae**

　　Fig. 90. 3 spp. in genus *Ephemera*.

— Gills not held over the back. Mandibles not projecting in front of the head. If burrowing, of small size . . 11

11. Gills extended out sideways. Large nymphs clinging to
    stones .   . POTAMANTHIDAE **Potamanthus luteus** (Linn.)

    Fig. 91. The only recent records are from the R.Usk and the
    R.Wye.

— Gills hidden beneath gill-covers. Living in mud and vegetable debris   .   .   .   .   .   . **Caenidae**

    Fig. 92. 5 spp. in genus *Caenis* and *Brachycercus harrisella*
    Curtis.

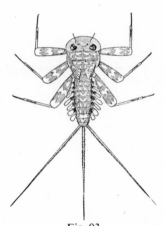

Fig. 93
Ecdyonurus venosus (Fabricius) 12 mm long (from l.s.)

12. Body flat with very broad head and femora. Gills consist-
    ing of a flat plate and a tuft of filaments. Rather large or
    moderate-sized nymphs found clinging closely to stones
    Ecdyonuridae

    Fig. 93. 10 spp. in *Ecdyonurus* (4), *Rhithrogena* (2), and
    Heptagenia (4).
    Macan, T. T. (1949), *Ent. mon. Mag.* **85,** 64–70 (*Ecdyonurus*)
    and (1958), *Ent. Gaz.* **9,** 83–92 (*Rhithrogena* and *Heptagenia*)..

— Body not flat, neither head nor femora particularly broad.
   Gills not thus. Habit not thus .   .   .   .   , 13

13. Gills lying on the back (i.e. in outline a specimen without its gills appears just the same from above as one with its gills). Tails short and with scattered bristles. Poor swimmers clinging to weed or living under stones

    Ephemerellidae

    Fig. 94.   2 spp. in genus *Ephemerella*.

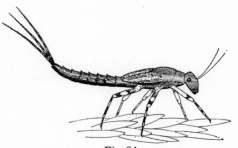

Fig. 94
Ephemerella ignita (Poda) 7 mm long (from l.s.)

— Gills attached to the sides of the body. If the tails are short, they are fringed with a close-set row of hairs. Moderate to good swimmers   14

14. Tails long with scattered bristles. Gills of two blades, bulbous at the base and with a long tapering portion; of two strap-like filaments; or of several filaments. Laboured swimming   .   .   .   .   .   **Leptophlebiidae**

    6 spp., 2 in *Leptophlebia* (figs. 95, 96), 3 in *Paraleptophlebia* (fig. 97), *Habrophlebia fusca* (Curtis) (fig. 98).

— Tails shorter with a close-set line of hairs along the inner margin of the outer ones and both margins of the inner ones. Gills not like this. Quick swimming .   .   . 15

15. Last but one abdominal segment and two or three before it produced into spines at the hind corners. (Tails all of the same length) .   .   .   .   .   . **Siphlonuridae**

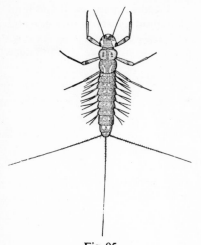

Fig. 96
Gill of *Leptophlebia*
sp. 7 mm long

Fig. 97
Gill of *Paraleptophlebia*
sp. 5 mm long

Fig. 95
Paraleptophlebia submarginata (Stephens)
7 mm long (from l.s.)

Fig. 98
Gill of *Habrophlebia fusca*
1·8 mm long

Figs. 99 and 100. 4 spp., 3 in genus *Siphlonurus* and *Ameletus inopinatus* Eaton.

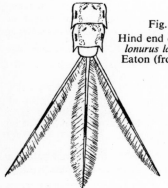

Fig. 99
Hind end of *Siph-lonurus lacustris*
Eaton (from l.s.)

Fig. 100
Hind end of *Ameletus inopinatus*
(from l.s.)

— No abdominal segments produced into spines at the hind corners. (Tails of the same length in *Cloeon*, *Procloeon* and *Centroptilum*, but middle one shorter than the outer ones in *Baetis*) . . . . . . **Baetidae**

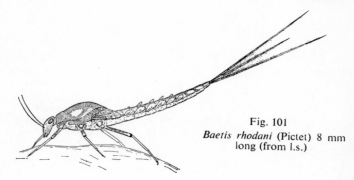

Fig. 101
Baetis rhodani (Pictet) 8 mm long (from l.s.)

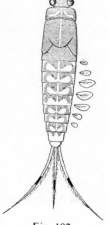

Fig. 102
Baetis scambus Eaton 6 mm long

14 spp., 9 in *Baetis* (figs. 101 and 102), 2 in *Cloeon* (figs. 103 and 104), 2 in *Centroptilum* (figs. 105 and 106) and *Procloeon pseudorufulum* Kimmins (fig. 107).

16. Slender nymphs, with three plates, flat or triangular in cross-section, at the end of the abdomen (figs. 108 and 112) 17

— Robust nymphs, with the abdomen ending in three triangular points (figs. 113 and 114) . . . 19

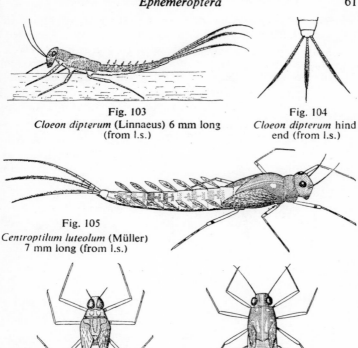

Fig. 103
Cloeon dipterum (Linnaeus) 6 mm long
(from l.s.)

Fig. 104
Cloeon dipterum hind
end (from l.s.)

Fig. 105
Centroptilum luteolum (Müller)
7 mm long (from l.s.)

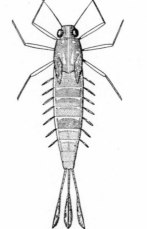

Fig. 106
Centroptilum pennulatum Eaton
9 mm long (from l.s.)

Fig. 107
Procloeon pseudorufulum Kimmins
7 mm long (from l.s.)

17. The two lateral plates at the end of the body triangular in cross-section, the middle one flat. Labium with a deep cleft in the front margin (fig. 108). Relatively large nymphs with long antennae, long legs and long bodies, found buried in mud or sand . . . . **Agriidae** (Calopterygidae)

> Fig. 108. 2 spp. in genus *Agrion*. (This name used to be applied to what is now *Coenagrion*, the present genus being known as *Calopteryx*).

— All plates flat. Labium with a shallow cleft or no cleft. Smaller nymphs, with less ungainly proportions, found in vegetation 18

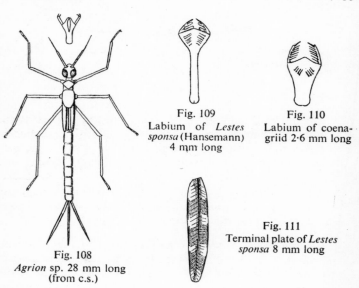

Fig. 109
Labium of *Lestes sponsa* (Hansemann) 4 mm long

Fig. 110
Labium of coena-griid 2·6 mm long

Fig. 111
Terminal plate of *Lestes sponsa* 8 mm long

Fig. 108
Agrion sp. 28 mm long
(from c.s.)

18. Labium with a long narrow basal portion (fig. 109). Terminal plates long, broad, rounded at the tip and heavily pigmented (fig. 111) . . . . **Lestidae**

> 2 spp. in genus *Lestes*.

— Labium with a short broad basal portion (fig. 110). Terminal plates smaller, usually pointed at the tip and usually not heavily pigmented .   .   .   **Coenagriidae**

Fig. 112. 13 spp. in 6 genera.

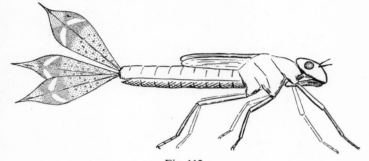

Fig. 112
Pyrrhosoma nymphula (Sulzer) 12 mm long (from l.s.)

19. Labium flat, the side pieces small with big spines at the end; or labium concave with a two-pointed projection in the middle of the front margin, the side pieces large, concave and triangular with the inner margin deeply and irregularly toothed .   .   .   .   **Aeshnidae**

Fig. 113. 10 spp., *Aeshna* (6), *Cordulegaster boltonii* (Donovan), *Gomphus vulgatissimus* (Linnaeus), *Anax imperator* Leach, *Brachytron pratense* (Müller).

— Labium concave, with no projection or a single, pointed projection in the middle of the front margin; the side pieces large, concave and triangular, with small regular teeth along the inner margin .   .   .   .   **Libellulidae**

Fig. 114. 6 British genera: *Orthetrum* (2 spp.), *Oxygastra curtisii* (Dale), *Libellula* (3 spp.), *Sympetrum* (6 spp.), *Leucorrhinia dubia* Van der Linden, *Somatochlora* (2 spp.), and *Cordulia aenea* (Linnaeus). Nymphs usually buried in the mud.

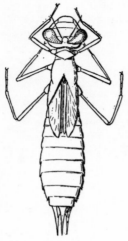

Fig. 113
Aeshna sp. 40 mm long
(from c.s.)

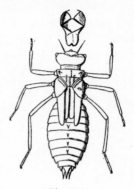

Fig. 114
Libellula quadrimaculata
Linn. 25 mm long
(from c.s.)

Key 4c pt. 2.

(*from p.* 50)

1. Small insects living on the surface of the water and having at the hind end a forked organ by means of which they can spring in the air   .   .   Springtails Order **Collembola**

> Figs. 115–117. Most Collembola live in damp places, under dead leaves, in moss, and so on. A few are definitely aquatic, but a number of others live very close to the water's edge in sphagnum or other vegetation and venture on to the water now and then. It is therefore difficult to decide which to include in a work on freshwater animals, and none of the authorities agree.

Fig. 115
Hydropodura aquatica (Linn.)
(1 mm long)

Fig. 116
Sminthurides sp. (0·5 mm long)

Fig. 117
Proisotoma sp. (5 mm long)

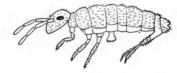

Heymons, R. and H. (1909), S.W.F.D. 7, 16 pp. (aquatic spp. only, 11 in all and a number of varieties).

Handschin, E. (1929), T.W.D. 16, 150 pp. (all species, 196 altogether).

Gisin, H. (1944), *Verh. naturf. Gesell. Basel.* **55**, 1–130 (all species; this key is not illustrated).

— Small, medium-sized or large insects without a springing organ and living in the water 2

2. Abdomen ending in a single tail; sides of abdominal segments with long, unbranched, jointed, filamentous gills beset with fine hairs. With large jaws projecting in front of the head. When disturbed it has the habit of raising its abdomen and proceeding backwards with its jaws open. Living in mud .   .   .   . Order **Megaloptera**

Fig. 118. 2 spp. in genus *Sialis*.

Kimmins, D. E. (1962), F.B.A.S.P. 8.

— Not thus 3

3. Mandibles and maxillae modified into long finely tapering stylites projecting a long way in front of head.

Order **Neuroptera**

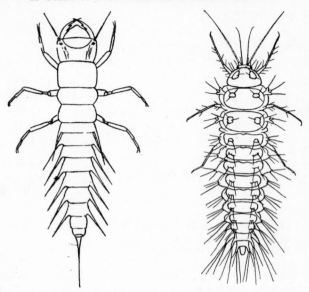

Fig. 118
Sialis lutaria (Linn.) 17 mm long
(from l.s.)

Fig. 119
Sisyra sp. 5 mm long (after
Kimmins)

Sisyra (3 spp., fig. 119) is found living inside sponges, *Osymylus fulvicephalus* (Scopoli) in moss at the edge of streams.
Kimmins, D. E. (1962), F.B.A.S.P. 8.

— Mouthparts of typical biting type   4

4. With a pair of legs ending in hooks at the hind end of the abdomen. Either dwelling in a case or spinning a net to catch current-borne material in weeds or under stones; or (1 genus) free-living in running water. Never with un-jointed legs on the abdomen   .   Order TRICHOPTERA 5

Key to genera in Hickin, N. E. (1946), *Trans. R. Ent. Soc.*

Lond. **97**, 187-212, and in Hickin, N. E. (1967). *Caddis larvae*. London: Hutchinson. *xii*+476. Gives keys to the larvae as far as they are known.

— Not thus 23

5. Larvae dwelling in cases, in tunnels on some solid surface, or in sponges. Last two segments short (fig. 128) . 9

— Larvae not dwelling in cases, tunnels or sponges; free-living or living in nets that are spun to catch food. Last two segments long (figs. 120–123) 6

6. With tufts of gills on the abdominal segments . . 7

— No gills except sometimes on the last segment . . 8

7. Gills on the sides of the abdominal segments. Mesonotum and metanotum soft, like the abdominal segments. Greenish larva with a narrow head. A free-living predator dwelling in streams . . . . **Rhyacophila**

Fig. 120. (Rhyacophilidae) 4 spp.
Mackereth, J. C. (1954), *Proc. R. Ent. Soc. Lond.* (A) **29**, 147–152.

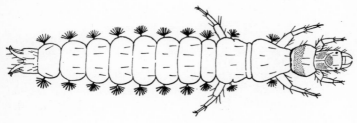

Fig. 120
Rhyacophila sp. 20 mm long

— Gills on the underside of the abdominal segments. Mesonotum and metanotum hard. Brownish larva without a
particularly narrow head. A net-spinner found in running
water   .   .   .   .   .   .   **Hydropsychidae**

Fig. 121   10 spp., 8 in *Hydropsyche*.

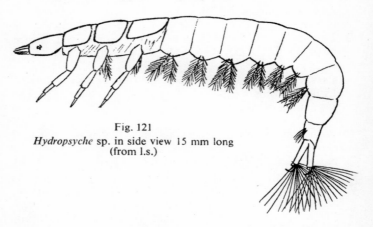

Fig. 121
Hydropsyche sp. in side view 15 mm long
(from l.s.)

8. Orange or yellow-brown heads without dark markings.
Fronto-clypeus (the piece in the middle of the head) rather
narrow as in fig. 122   .   .   .   .   **Philopotamidae**

4 spp. in 3 genera.

— Head and pronotum dull greenish or brownish with black
dots. Fronto-clypeus wider, as in fig. 123

Polycentropidae
13 spp. in 5 genera. Edington, J. M. (1964) *Proc. zool. Soc.
Lond.* **143**, 281–300.

9. Larvae dwelling in tunnels covered with fine silt and debris
and attached to some solid surface. *Ecnomus tenellus*
Raub. sometimes found in sponges   .   . **Psychomyidae**

12 spp. in 5 genera.

— Larvae dwelling in movable cases **10**

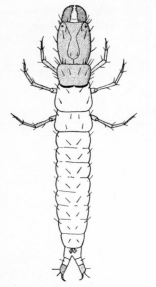

Fig. 122
Philopotamus sp. 15 mm long

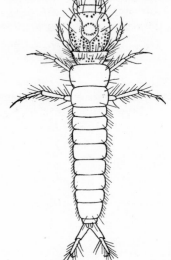

Fig. 123
Plectrocnemia sp. 15 mm long

10. Larvae which swim with the aid of long bristles on the long
back legs 11

— Larvae which crawl 12

11. Long, neat tapering case of vegetable fragments arranged
spirally . . . . . . **Triaenodes**

    (Leptoceridae) 2 spp.

— Case quill-like, not made out of vegetable fragments
Setodes

    (Leptoceridae) 5 spp.

12. Mesonotum (the top part of the middle thoracic segment) soft (fig. 124), or with small hard plates which appear as darker areas bearing bristles 13

— Mesonotum hard (fig. 128) or more or less completely covered by large plates 15

13. Large larvae with yellow heads marked with two black stripes. Cases made of vegetable fragments laid longitudinally and wound spirally . . . . **Phryganeidae**
Fig. 124. 9 spp. in 4 genera.

Bray, R. P. (1967), *J. Zool.* **153**, 223-244.

— Small larvae with uniformly dark heads. Cases somewhat oval in outline and made of coarse sand grains . . 14

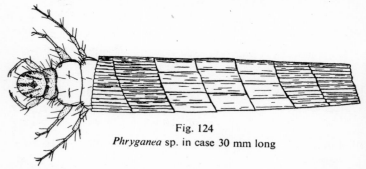

Fig. 124
Phryganea sp. in case 30 mm long

14. Mesonotum and metanotum soft . . **Glossosoma**
(Rhyacophilidae) 3 spp.

— Mesonotum and metanotum each with two plates
Agapetus
(Rhyacophilidae) 3 spp.
Mackereth, J. C. (1956), *Proc. R. Ent. Soc. Lond.* (A) **31**, 167-172 (both genera).

15. Plates of pronotum and mesonotum of such shape and arrangement that they form a roughly circular hard area

(fig. 125). Case of sand grains with a row of stones attached to each side 16

— Neither plates nor case like this 17

16. Of the three plates on either side of the mesonotum, the middle one is triangular and does not reach the front edge of the segment . **Goera pilosa** Fabricius

(Sericostomatidae.)

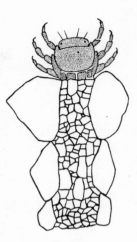

— The middle plate quadrangular and reaching the front edge of the segment . . . **Silo**

Fig. 125. 2 spp. (Sericostomatidae).

Fig. 125
Silo sp. in case 6 mm long

17. Metanotum apparently entirely soft like those of the abdominal segments (there may be some tiny plates lying against those of the mesonotum and appearing to belong to that segment) 18

— Metanotum with some hard plates which may appear to be no more than black spots each bearing a hair . . 19

18. Larval case of sand grains with wing-like lateral projections . . . . **Molannidae**

Fig. 126. 2 spp. in *Molanna.*

— Larval case with no lateral expansions (many are made of sand grains or small stones) . . **Beraeidae** (4 spp.), rest of **Leptoceridae** (23 spp.), part of **Sericostomatidae** (2 spp.)

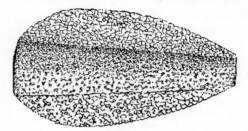

Fig. 126
Case of *Molanna* sp. (20 mm long)

19. Plates of metanotum, two in number, covering the notum completely. Tiny larvae (up to 7 mm long) which live in large seed-like or flask-shaped cases that may be entirely of secreted material or may be covered with stones or vegetable fragments . . . . . **Hydroptilidae**

 Fig. 127. 28 spp. in 8 genera.

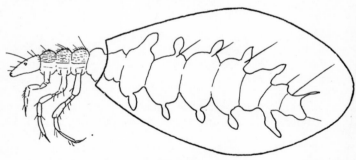

Fig. 127
Ithytrichia lamellaris (3 mm long) Eaton (after Wesenberg-Lund)

— More than two metanotal plates not covering the notum completely 20

20. Four metanotal plates 21

— Six metanotal plates 22

21. Two metanotal plates at the side, a long rectangular one at the front and a long spindle-shaped one at the back (fig. 128). (Case of sand grains)

(ODONTOCERIDAE) **Odontocerum albicorne** (Scopoli)

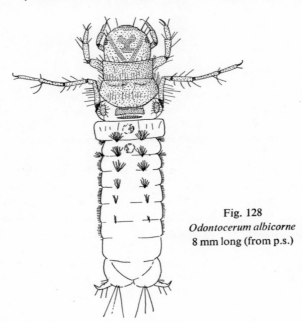

Fig. 128
Odontocerum albicorne
8 mm long (from p.s.)

— Metanotal sclerites along the hind margin (fig. 129)
(Sericostomatidae) **Brachycentrus subnubilus** Curtis

22. Four median metanotal plates very small and with only one hair arising from each; or with median metanotal plates larger, each bearing more than one hair, and with 8 mesonotal sclerites . . . **Lepidostomatinae**

4 spp. in 3 genera (Sericostomatidae).

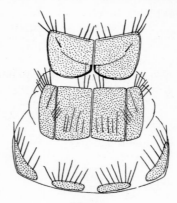

Fig. 129
Pro-, meso- and metanotum of *Brachycentrus subnubilus*

— Four median metanotal plates not very small, each bearing several hairs and with mesonotum divided into two by central longitudinal line . . . . **Limnephilidae**

Fig. 130.   55 spp., 25 in genus *Limnephilus* (*Limnophilus*).

Many of the common pond species belong to the genus *Limnephilus*. The case is often made of short lengths of vegetable matter stuck on across the long axis of the tube and it may have a characteristic appearance; but identification of

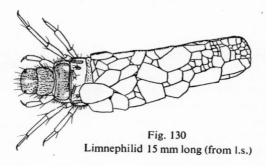

Fig. 130
Limnephilid 15 mm long (from l.s.)

caddis larvae from their cases is always uncertain, because the material used may vary according to what is available. It may, moreover, change with the season or with the age of the larvae.

23. With unjointed legs on abdominal segments 3, 4, 5, 6 and 10. Usually living in a case made of two pieces of leaf held together by silk, or boring into the tissues of plants. 5 spp. . . . . Moths Order **Lepidoptera**

— Without legs on the abdominal segments except in *Enochrus* which has them on segments 3, 4, 5, 6, 7. Diverse larvae, but without any of the combinations of characteristics so far mentioned
Order COLEOPTERA 24

Böving, A. G., and Craighead, F. C. (1931), *Ent. amer.* **11**, nos. 1–4.

24. Femur, tibia and tarsus (the last three segments of the leg) relatively well developed and generally long, with one or two distinct movable claws at the end of the tarsus . 25

— Legs with not more than two long segments and a single claw-shaped segment at the tip. (Different authorities have different views about which segments are fused with which) . . . 29

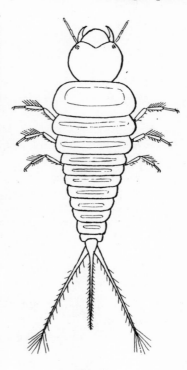

Fig. 131

Hygrobia hermanni (12 mm long)
(after Bertrand)

Fig. 132
Haliplid 7 mm long

25. Ventral abdominal gills. Three long "tails" (fig. 131) **Hygrobiidae** *Hygrobia* (*Pelobius*) *hermanni* (*tardus*) (Fab.)

— Abdominal gills, if present, lateral. "Tails" never long, nor more than two in number . 26

26. Long thin larvae. Hind margins of abdominal terga produced into triangular spines. Abdomen terminating in a long, tapering tail-process. Tarsi with one claw. (In *Peltodytes* (*Cnemidotus*) *caesus* (Duftsch.) long thread-like processes spring from the abdominal terga, and the abdomen ends in two long tail-like processes) . **Haliplidae**

Fig. 132. 18 spp., all but two in the genus *Haliplus*.

— More robust larvae. Abdomen without spines or processes. Usually two small tail-like processes (cerci) at the end of the abdomen. Tarsi with two claws 27

27. Lateral abdominal gills. Four hooks at the end of the abdomen . . . . . . **Gyrinidae**

Fig. 133. 12 spp., all but two in the genus *Gyrinus*.

— No abdominal gills. No hooks at the end of the abdomen
DYTISCIDAE 28

28. Body cylindrical, tapering at the hind end. Legs short.

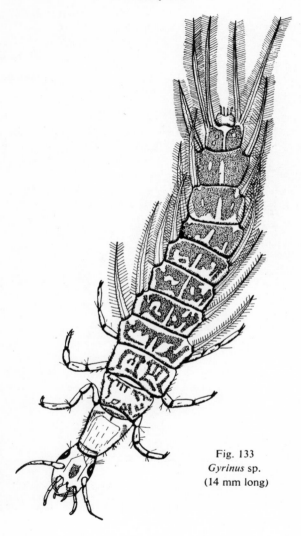

Fig. 133
Gyrinus sp.
(14 mm long)

Head globular and without a projection in front. Cerci short or very short. Burrowing larvae **Noterinae**

Fig. 134. 2 spp. (Family Noteridae of some authors.)

— Body spindle-shaped. Legs long or moderately long. Head flat (fig. 135), or globular and with a projection in front (fig. 136,

Fig. 134
Noterus sp. 7 mm long and foreleg (after Wesenberg-Lund)

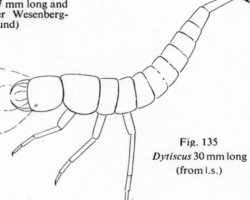

Fig. 135
Dytiscus 30 mm long
(from l.s.)

Hydroporini). Cerci longer. Swimming and crawling larvae . . . . **Dytiscinae**

108 spp. Bertrand, H. (1928), Les larves et nymphes des Dytiscides, Hygrobiides et Haliplides. *Encyclopédie Entomologique* **10**, Paris: Lechevalier.

29. Body curved ventrally. Grub-like larvae living permanently attached to the roots or stems of plants, from the air spaces of which they obtain oxygen

CHRYSOMELIDAE **Donaciinae**

Fig. 137. 20 spp.

— Body straight or more or less so. Larvae not attached to plants and not obtaining oxygen from them . . 30

30. Larvae without gills retractable within a pocket at the hind end of the body. Mostly soft-skinned larvae progressing somewhat after the manner of a maggot . **Hydrophilidae**

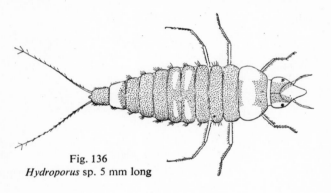

Fig. 136
Hydroporus sp. 5 mm long

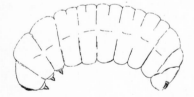

Fig. 137
Donacia sp. 10 mm long
(from l.s.)

This family, with seven sub-families, is not entirely aquatic, the larvae of some species living in dung, decaying fungi, damp soil, etc. They are diverse in form and structure. Many are elongate, and somewhat grub-like, with rela-

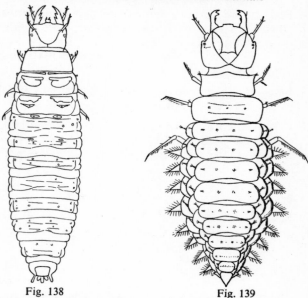

Fig. 138

Hydrobius fuscipes (Linn.) (10 mm long) (after Böving and Craighead)

Fig. 139

Spercheus emarginatus (Schaller) (8 mm long) (after Wesenberg-Lund)

tively short legs, and without any outstanding features (fig. 138); others have peculiar features, e.g.

Spercheus (Spercheinae) has abdominal segments with conical, gill-like projections (fig. 139).

Sphaeridium (Sphaeridiinae) has greatly reduced legs.

Enochrus (*Philhydrus*) (Hydrophilinae) has five abdominal prolegs.

Berosus (Hydrophilinae) has long simple gills on the abdominal segments (fig. 140).

Hydrochara caraboides (Linn.) (Hydrophilinae) has short lateral abdominal gills (fig. 141).

Hydrophilus piceus (Linn.) (Hydrophilinae) resembles a *Dytiscus* larva but is less graceful and active, and has short processes on the side of each abdominal segment.

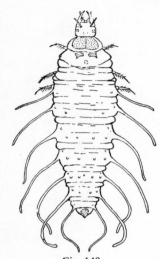
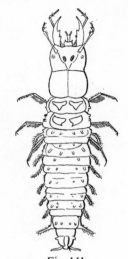

Fig. 140
Berosus sp. (6 mm long) (after Böving and Craighead)

Fig. 141
Hydrochara caraboides (25 mm long) (after Böving and Craighead)

Bøving, A. G. and Henriksen, K. L. (1938), *Vidensk. Medd. dansk. naturh. Foren. Kbh.* **102,** 27–162. (The paper is in English.)

— Larvae with gills retractable within a pocket at the hind end of the body. Hard-skinned larvae which walk on the bottom 31

31. Antennae long. No lid closing the terminal gill chamber; (larvae somewhat broad and flat) . . **Helodidae**
    Fig. 142. 13 spp. in 6 genera.

— Antennae short. Terminal gill chamber can be closed with a lid; (larvae broad and flat (fig. 143) or somewhat cylindrical (fig. 144)) . **Helminthidae** (Elmidae, Helmidae)
    11 spp. in 6 genera.
    Holland, D. G. (in prep.), F.B.A.S.P.
    The family Dryopidae (Parnidae) is often included here, but

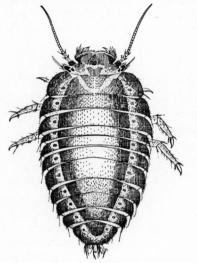

Fig. 142
Helodid 6 mm long

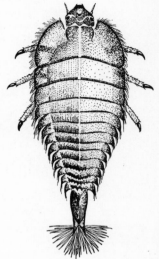

Fig. 143
Helmis maugei Bedel (3 mm long)

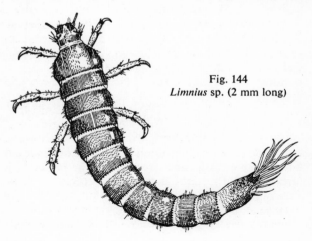

Fig. 144
Limnius sp. (2 mm long)

H. E. Hinton (1955, *Proc. Zool. Soc. Lond.* **125,** p. 566), writes: "I am aware of no authentic instance of larvae of these genera (*Dryops* and *Helichus*) being found actually in the water." The adults are aquatic.

Key 4c pt. 3

(from p. 50)

LEGLESS LARVAE (*Diptera*)

AMONG what are regarded as the more primitive Diptera, which in the adult stage generally have thin bodies and long legs, there are several families which are predominantly or entirely aquatic as larvae and possessed of distinct characteristics. Common to most is a distinct head, chitinized all round, attached to the body by a neck and not retractable into the body, as well as a rather slim and rigid form. The mouthparts are well developed and the mandibles work, generally in the horizontal plane, against each other. These families are the Simuliidae (Buffalo Gnats), Culicidae (Mosquitoes), Chironomidae and Ceratopogonidae (Midges), Thaumaleidae, and Psychodidae (Moth flies).

It is possible to present a key to these with some confidence, for the immature stages are well known. Among the higher Diptera—that is, those that are compact and short-legged as adults and whose larvae are grub-like with a progressive deterioration of the head and mouthparts till the only hard parts are a pair of hooks moving in the vertical plane—there are few families wholly aquatic when young. The larvae often live in such places as dung, damp soil, rotting vegetation and other places from which a transition to an aquatic life is quite simple, and may have been achieved by several species in one family independently. Some larvae show little or no modification;

others have undergone quite a lot and are not easily recognizable as such when placed among close relatives. A large number of these larvae are unknown, and therefore I have not attempted to make a key; to do so would be misleading.

The heading to this key is "legless larvae" because jointed ₁egs such as other immature insects possess are absent, but some larvae have unjointed projections from the body known as "prolegs".

Since they do not come the way of the collector using the oɪdinary methods, larvae that mine in the tissues of aquatic plants have been left out. Had they been included it would have been necessary to include also some Curculionidae (Weevils) of the order Coleoptera.

In compiling this section, I have made extensive reference to Wesenberg-Lund (1943) and Bertrand (1954) of the authors quoted at the beginning, and also to W. Hennig (1948, 1950, 1952), *Die Larvenform der Diptera* parts 1, 2 and 3, Berlin: Akademie Verlag. Vaillant, F. (1955), Recherches sur la faune madicole de France, de Corse, et d'Afrique du Nord, *Mem. Mus. Hist. nat. Paris.* **11,** 1–252, though not taxonomic, contains useful illustrations and references.

Key

1. Larvae dumb-bell-shaped. With numerous little hooks on a basal pad and on a proleg near the head. Maxillae provided with long hairs which strain particles from the water. Living in exposed places in flowing water, attached by the basal pad to a web spun over the surface of a rock or plant **Simuliidae** (Melusinidae)

   Fig. 145.   19 spp.   Davies, L. (1968), F.B.A.S.P. 23.

— Larvae not dumb-bell-shaped. Without hooks on a basal pad. Mouthparts of other type   2

2. Thoracic segments fused into a mass of greater diameter than the abdomen. (Living at the surface of the water with

the last pair of spiracles open to the air, except for one species which obtains air from plant tissues and two unmistakable genera with hydrostatic swim-bladders living in the open water)   3

— Each thoracic segment distinct, so that there is little difference between the thoracic and the abdominal segments .   .   . 6

3. Larvae obtaining oxygen from the air or from plants. Opaque. The labrum provided with close-set bristles, by constant motion of which a current is maintained through the other mouthparts, which, being provided with bristles, strain out fine particles
   Mosquitoes CULICIDAE Culicinae 4

   Marshall, J. F. (1938), *The British Mosquitoes*, Brit. Mus. (N.H.).

Fig. 145
Simulium sp. 7 mm long
(from l.s.)

— Larvae hanging motionless in midwater most of the time and obtaining oxygen from solution. Transparent or semitransparent except for the black air-sacs, of which a pair lies in the thorax and a pair near the end of the abdomen. Carnivorous, the prey being seized by the antennae
                              CULICIDAE **Chaoborinae** (Corethrinae)

   2 spp. in *Mochlonyx* (fig. 146) and 4 in *Chaoborus* (fig. 147).
   Peus, F. (1934), *Arch. Hydrobiol.* **27**, 641–668.

4. At the end of the abdomen there is a pointed projection around the opening of the breathing-tubes; this pierces

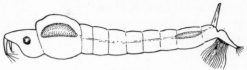

Fig. 146
Mochlonyx sp. 6 mm long

Fig. 147
Chaoborus sp. 9 mm long (from l.s.)

Fig. 148
Taeniorhynchus
richiardii
6mm long (after
Wesenberg-
Lund)

the roots or stems of plants to tap the air-channels and the larva is fixed most of the time (fig. 148)

Taeniorhynchus richiardii (Ficalbi)

— Larvae obtaining oxygen at the surface . 5

5. Breathing-tubes ending in a saucer-shaped organ raised only slightly above the general level of the abdomen; body hanging parallel with the water surface . . **Anopheles**

Fig. 149. 4 spp.

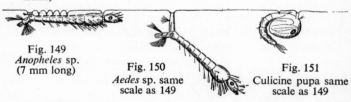

Fig. 149
Anopheles sp.
(7 mm long)

Fig. 150
Aedes sp. same
scale as 149

Fig. 151
Culicine pupa same
scale as 149

— Breathing-tubes at the end of a conical projection—the siphon; body hanging head downwards at an angle to the surface . . . . **Culicini**

Fig. 150. 4 British genera: *Orthopodomyia* (1 sp.), *Theobaldia* (7 spp.), *Aedes* (14 spp.) and *Culex* (3 spp.).

6. Larvae living at the edge of the water, and commonly found bent into a characteristic U-shape. Mouthparts and opening of the breathing-tubes as in *Anopheles*, to which there is a superficial resemblance, though the three distinct thoracic segments afford an immediate distinction. Leg-like projections with hooks at the tip on the abdominal segments 1 and 2. Long bristles on the first thoracic and last abdominal segment . . . CULICIDAE **Dixinae**

Fig. 152. 13 spp. in genus *Dixa*.

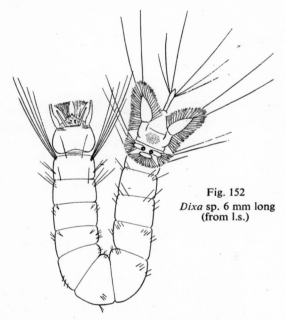

Fig. 152
Dixa sp. 6 mm long
(from l.s.)

— Without the above combination of characters . . 7

7. No open spiracles 8

— A pair of spiracles opening on the thorax, and another pair
   opening at the end of the abdomen. (A single proleg on the
   prothorax. Last segment elongate and with spines at the
   tip. Segments with dorsal chitinous saddles)

                          Thaumaleidae (Orphnephilidae)

   Fig. 153.   3 spp. living at the surface among vegetation or at
   the edges of stones.

Fig. 153
Thaumalea sp. 6 mm long (from p.s.)

8. Larvae with prolegs on first thoracic and last abdominal
   segments but without lateral projections and hairs. (Body
   somewhat rigid, with all segments usually of similar
   diameter. Head of characteristic shape. In addition to
   sausage-like "anal gills" on last segment, similar "gills"

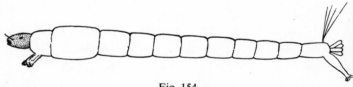

Fig. 154
Chironomid 6 mm long (from l.s.)

often on last segment but one. Colour ranges from bright
red, through pink and yellowish to green, some species
with blue bands)   .   .   **Chironomidae** (Tendipedidae)

   Fig. 154.   Nearly 400 spp. Though rather uniform in structure,
   this group is extremely diverse in habitat and may be found
   on almost any substratum in freshwater.

— If there are prolegs at back and front, the segments are produced laterally and armed with hairs (figs. 156 and 157) 9

9. Twenty-six chitinous plates bearing hairs on the dorsal surface. Some species heavily encrusted with lime

Pericoma (PSYCHODIDAE)

Fig. 155. 24 spp. occurring in clumps of damp moss, algal mats, dead leaves, etc., at the margins of streams and trickles. Satchell, G. H. (1949), *Trans. R. Ent. Soc. Lond.* **100**, 411–447.

(*Psychoda* (16 spp.) is similar, though the dorsal plates may be fewer and less hairy. The larvae are not aquatic, being found in rotting vegetation, dung and the trickling filters of sewage works.)

Satchell, G. H. (1947), *Parasitology* **38**, 51–69.

— Without chitinous plates on the back

CERATOPOGONIDAE (Heleidae) 10

There are just over 100 species in this family, but it is impossible to say how many are aquatic. Some genera and some species in genera named below live in dung, moss, exudations from wounds in trees and other damp places. *Forcipomyia*, which has prothoracic legs, is stated by Wesenberg-Lund and Bertrand to have no aquatic species, but Vaillant records three in water-films, none of them, however, on the British list. Its mouthparts point downwards, not forwards, as do those of chironomids.

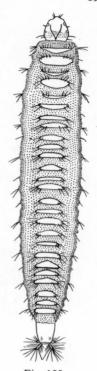

Fig. 155

Pericoma pseudo exquisita Tonnoir 4 mm long (after Satchell)

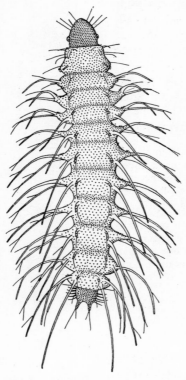

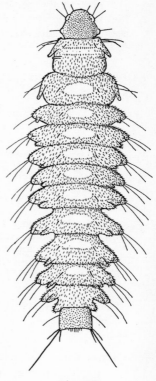

Fig. 156
Atrichopogon sp. 3 mm long
(after Anker Nielsen)

Fig. 157
Atrichopogon sp. 3 mm long
(after Anker Nielsen)

10. Larvae with lateral projections (figs. 156 and 157)
   Atrichopogon

   12 spp.   Nielsen, A. (1951), *K. danske. vidensk. Selsk. Skr.* **6,**
   1–95.

   Without lateral projections   11

11. Larvae long thin and snake-like, super-
ficially like a nematode worm (fig. 158).
No prolegs
Culicoides, Ceratopogon, Bezzia, etc.

> Kettle, D. S., and Lawson, J. W. H.
> (1952), The early stages of British biting
> midges *Culicoides* (Latreille) (Diptera:
> Ceratopogonidae) and allied genera. *Bull.
> Ent. Res.* **43**, 421–467.

— Larvae less long and thin. Prolegs on
last abdominal segment . **Dashyhelea**

Larvae of Tipulidae (craneflies) occupy
all sorts of places, some being the familiar
lawn-pest known as the leatherjacket, others
being truly aquatic. Although the family
belongs to the "lower" Diptera, the head is
less complete than in the families so far
considered and can be withdrawn into the
body. The mouthparts, however, have jaws

Fig. 158
Ceratopogonid
4 mm long
(from l.s.)

that lie opposite and work from side to side against each other.

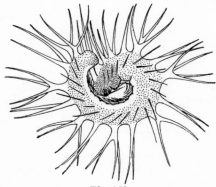

Fig. 159
Phalacrocera replicata (20 mm long) (from l.s.)

92 *A Guide to Freshwater Invertebrate Animals*

Phalacrocera replicata (Linn.) (fig. 159), with long processes from the back, which make it look like a sprig of the moss in which it lives, is one of the most distinct of all larvae. *Triogma trisulcata* (Schummel) and *Diogma glabrata* (Meigen) are similar except that the processes are short and triangular. The rest

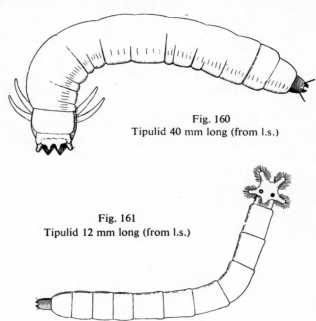

Fig. 160
Tipulid 40 mm long (from l.s.)

Fig. 161
Tipulid 12 mm long (from l.s.)

are all grub-like. In the Tipulinae the spiracles generally open into a depression at the back surrounded by six hairy processes (fig. 160). In the Limoniinae (or Limnobiidae) there are usually fewer processes. *Pedicia*, fairly common in stony streams, has two processes at the hind end, two pairs of gills, four pairs of prolegs, and a habit of inflating and deflating the last but one segment (fig. 162). *Dicranota*, similar but smaller and more active, and also found in streams, has five pairs of prolegs (fig. 163).

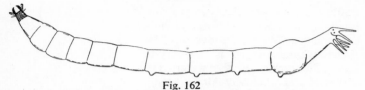

Fig. 162
Pedicia rivosa (Linn.) half-grown specimen 30 mm long (from l.s.)

Close to the Tipulidae are the PTYCHOPTERIDAE (Liriopidae), a family with but seven species. The small head is complete. The body is cylindrical at first, with thickenings at the hind end of the fourth to eighth abdominal segments, and then

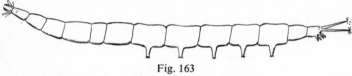

Fig. 163
Dicranota sp. 12 mm long (from l.s.)

tapers to end in a long telescopic respiratory process (fig. 164), which is characteristic. The species illustrated is found in woodland pools with dead leaves at the bottom.

It is logical to take next another larva with a long telescopic tail, the rat-tailed maggot of the genus *Tubifera* (*Eristalis*)

Fig. 164
Ptychoptera contaminata (Linn.) (70 mm long) (after Wesenberg-Lund)

(fig. 165) (SYRPHIDAE). The body is cylindrical, with seven prolegs. The head is much reduced, if indeed the animal can be said to have a head at all, and the mouthparts are surrounded by a sort of hood. Ten species inhabit dung-hill pools, sewage

outflows and other places highly pol-
luted with organic matter, crawling
through the filth and extending their
tails to whatever length is necessary to
reach the surface of the water. The
larvae of several closely related genera
have the same form. Less well known is
the genus *Chrysogaster* (5 spp.), whose
grub-like larva pierces the roots of
plants with its distinctive short, sharp,
dark breathing tube (fig. 166).

A third type of larva with a respiratory tail, which, however, is shorter,
less telescopic and divided into two
towards the tip, is that of *Ephydra*

Fig. 165
Tubifera
sp. (15 mm long)
(from l.s.)

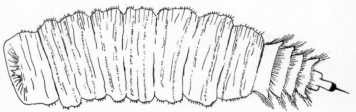

Fig. 166
Chrysogaster sp. 8 mm long (from l.s.)

(4 spp.), often found in brackish water. There are eight prolegs,
the last longer than the rest (fig. 167). Other members of the
family (EPHYDRIDAE) are less distinctive, some lacking prolegs,

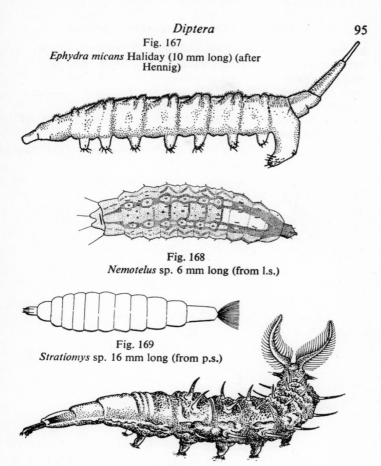

Fig. 167
Ephydra micans Haliday (10 mm long) (after Hennig)

Fig. 168
Nemotelus sp. 6 mm long (from l.s.)

Fig. 169
Stratiomys sp. 16 mm long (from p.s.)

Fig. 170
Atherix sp. 15 mm long (from l.s.)

but there is generally some indication of a double respiratory tube at the hind end.

The family STRATIOMYIDAE, with some fifty species, has several genera in which the larvae are aquatic and, as far as is known, they all possess the following distinctive features: a flattened body; a complete head distinctly narrower than the body and only slightly retractable within it; a leathery integument; a posterior opening to the breathing-tubes which is often slit-like and surrounded by hairs (figs 168 and 169). *Stratiomys* (4 spp.) is found in ponds and ditches. *Oxycera* (*Hermione*) occurs in water-films.

> Vaillant, F. (1952), Les larves d'*Hermione*. *Trav. Lab. Hydrobiol. Grenoble* **43, 44,** 23–38.

In the family RHAGIONIDAE (Leptidae) only the genus *Atherix* (3 spp.) has an aquatic larva as far as is known. This is unmistakable with its tapering forepart, well-developed prolegs, triangular projections on the abdominal segments and terminal appendages (fig. 170). One species at least is found on stony bottoms in swiftly flowing water.

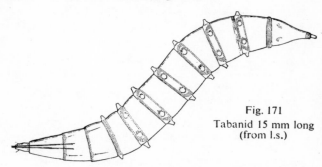

Fig. 171
Tabanid 15 mm long
(from l.s.)

Fig. 171 shows a larva of the family TABANIDAE. Its tapering form and the eight pseudopods on each thickened ring between the segments make it quite distinctive, especially in life, when the continual eversion and inversion of the pseudopods can be seen, but, until more of the species have been described, it would be unwise to try to set out characters diagnostic of the whole family.

Larvae of *Sepedon* and *Tetanocera* (SCIOMYZIDAE or Tetanoceridae) have thickenings round the body like those of

Tabanidae, and on them wart-like projections. The end of the last segment is surrounded by conical lobes. The larvae feed on snails.

Finally, there are some little-known families for which it is not possible to do much more than present illustrations of the few species that have been described. Larvae of DOLICHOPODIDAE may have prolegs or no more than areas provided with rows of little hooks (fig. 172). The breathing-tubes open into a terminal

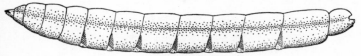

Fig. 172
Medetera sp. (after Hennig)

chamber surrounded by lobes, and the hind end has a square or concave appearance. This is not true of the EMPIDIDAE (figs. 173 and 174) whose breathing-tubes may not open to the surface at all.

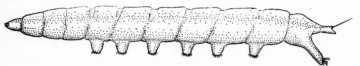

Fig. 173
Clinocera sp. (4 mm long) (after Hennig)

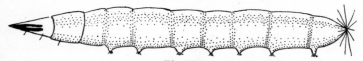

Fig. 174
Hemerodroma sp. (6 mm long) (after Brocher)

Limnophora (fig. 175), with its oblique hind end, is a rather distinctive member of the MUSCIDAE (Anthomyidae), but I have sometimes found in fresh water typical muscid maggots of a kind not pictured or mentioned in any work known to me.

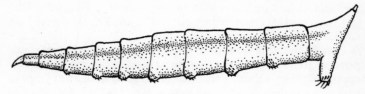

Fig. 175
Limnophora sp. (8 mm long) (after Wesenberg-Lund)

Key 4c pt. 4

(from p. 50)

ADULT BEETLES (*Coleoptera*) AND BUGS (*Hemiptera*)

1. Typical biting mouthparts. Antennae conspicuous. Fore
   wings modified as wing-cases (elytra), hard, sometimes
   sculptured with pits and ridges, never divided into areas,
   never absent .   .   .   .   Order COLEOPTERA 2

   Adult Coleoptera can be named from any of the standard
   handbooks: Fowler, W. W. (1887–1913), *Coleoptera of the
   British Islands*, 6 vols.; Joy, N. (1932), *A Practical Handbook
   of British Beetles*, 2 vols.; Balfour Browne, F. (1940, 1950,
   1958), *British Water Beetles*, R. S. 3 vols. (Haliplidae,
   Hygrobiidae, Dytiscidae, Gyrinidae, Hydrophilidae).

— With a beak, the mouthparts being modified for piercing
   and sucking, except in Corixidae (fig. 176), which sweep
   particles off the bottom and have a characteristic triangular
   head without a beak. Antennae small and inconspicuous
   except in surface-dwelling forms. Fore wings modified
   as wing-cases, never pitted or furrowed, clearly divided into
   areas (figs. 196, 197, 198, 200 and 201), sometimes absent
                                            Order HEMIPTERA 10

Aphelocheirus is found in large swift rivers, but all the other water-bugs are species of still or slow-flowing water.

Macan, T. T. (1965), F.B.A.S.P. 16.

2. Maxillary palps long, generally longer than the antennae. Antennae clubbed at the tip (fig. 177). Underside covered with hairs which hold a bubble of air when the beetle is submerged

Hydrophilidae

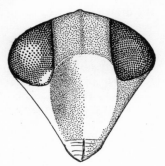

Fig. 176
Head of male *Corixa semistriata* Fieb. 2 mm long

This family includes the Great Black Water Beetle, *Hydrophilus* (*Hydrous*) *piceus* (Linn.) which, 1½ inches long, is one

Fig. 177
Hydrobius fuscipes (Linn.) 8 mm long (from m.s.)

of the largest British insects; *Hydrochara* (*Hydrous* or *Hydrophilus*) *caraboides*(Linn.), which is a little over ½ inch long and also black; and about one hundred small or tiny species. The first two and some of the others have swimming-hairs on the legs and can swim fairly well, but most do no more than crawl about in places densely overgrown with weeds, and some are not aquatic at all.

— Maxillary palps shorter than antennae. If the antennae are clubbed, it is the second joint that is swollen or the head is drawn out into a snout (fig. 183). If air is carried externally, it is usually not in a film on the underside of the body . 3

3. Middle and hind legs short and broad, functioning as paddles. Compound eyes divided into an upper and a lower portion, the latter on the underside of the head. Small, steely-black beetles dwelling on the surface of the water though capable of submerging when danger threatens
Whirligig Beetles . **Gyrinidae**

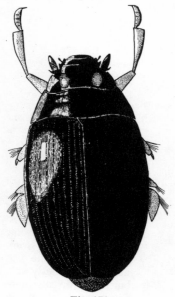

Fig. 178. 12 spp. Generally in groups; the habit of whirling round on the surface of the water at high speed and disappearing beneath it when the observer tries to catch them is distinctive.

— Middle and hind legs not short and broad. Compound eyes not in two parts. Not steely-black and not living on the surface of the water . 4

Fig. 178
Gyrinus sp. 6 mm long
(from m.s.)

4. Swimming beetles with swimming-hairs on the hind legs and a fairly unbroken outline (figs. 181 and 182). An air-bubble underneath the wings . 5

— Beetles which, though they may live all their lives submerged, have no obvious adaptations for an aquatic existence, the legs being without swimming-hairs and the outline not smooth (figs. 183–185) 7

5. Large plates covering the bases of the hind legs so that the point where they are attached to the body cannot be seen (fig. 179). (Head somewhat protruding. Hind legs not strongly flattened, moving alternately when being used for swimming. Small reddish-brown or yellowish-brown beetles often ornamented with pits) . . **Haliplidae**

   18 spp., generally in still water.

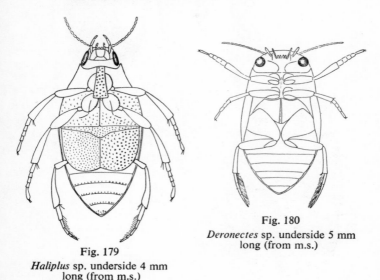

Fig. 179
Haliplus sp. underside 4 mm long (from m.s.)

Fig. 180
Deronectes sp. underside 5 mm long (from m.s.)

— No plates covering the bases of the hind legs, whose point of attachment to the body is visible (fig. 180) . . 6

6. Head and eyes somewhat protruding. Hind legs not strongly flattened. May squeak when caught. (A rather globular beetle, 8·5–10 mm long, reddish-yellow with black markings) (fig. 181) . **Hygrobia** (*Pelobius*) **hermanni** (Fab.) (*tarda* Herbst) (HYGROBIIDAE or Pelobiidae)

   In ponds in the south of England.

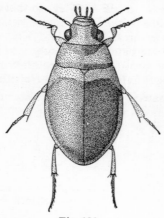

Fig. 181
Hygrobia hermanni 10 mm long
(from m.s.)

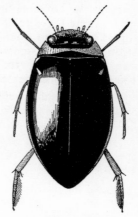

Fig. 182
Platambus maculatus (Linn.)
8 mm long (from m.s.)

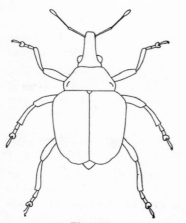

Fig. 183
Phytobius waltoni Boheman
2 mm long (after Joy)

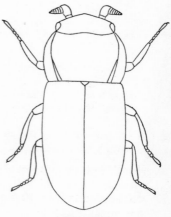

Fig. 184
Dryops ernesti Des Gozis 5·5 mm
long (after Joy)

— Head sunk in thorax and eyes not protruding, so that the front end has a smooth outline (fig. 182). Hind legs often strongly flattened. Never squeaks when caught. (When the beetle is swimming, the hind legs move together)

Dytiscidae

110 spp. of all sizes, most inhabiting still water. Carnivorous beetles, most of which are speedy and powerful swimmers, periodically visiting the surface, which they break with the tip of the abdomen to renew the store of air.

7. Head produced into a snout. Antennae bent in the middle and clubbed at the tip   .   .   Weevils **Curculionidae**

Fig. 183.   About 40 species of this large family live on aquatic plants and some of the adults spend a great part of their lives submerged.

— Head not produced into a snout. Antennae not bent in the middle and, if they are clubbed, it is the second joint that is swollen.   8

8. Tarsi apparently with four segments. Length 4·5–8·5 mm

Chrysomelidae

The sub-family Donaciinae (21 spp.) is characterized by a larva which takes air from the roots of water plants. Most of the adults are terrestrial, but those of *Macroplea* (*Haemonia*) (2 spp.) spend a great part of their lives under water.

— Tarsi with five segments. Length 1·2–5·5 mm. (Small inactive beetles found crawling among the stones in fast streams and the vegetation of stagnant water)   .   .   9

9. Second segment of antenna greatly enlarged (fig. 184). Last segment of tarsi not large and swollen at the tip

Dryopidae (Parnidae)

8 spp.

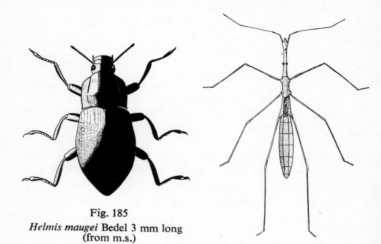

Fig. 185
Helmis maugei Bedel 3 mm long
(from m.s.)

Fig. 186
Hydrometra stagnorum (Linn.)
11 mm long (from m.s.)

— Antennae threadlike. Last segment of tarsi large and swollen at the tip (fig. 185)   .   **Helminthidae** (Elmidae, Helmidae)

   11 spp.

10. Living on the water. Body and legs long and narrow. Antennae conspicuous and longer than the head (figs. 186–194)   11

— Living in the water. Body and legs generally less long and narrow. Antennae shorter than the head and concealed beneath it (figs. 195–201)   15

11. Head many times longer than broad. Eyes situated some

distance from the anterior margin of the prothorax
Water-measurers or Water-gnats **Hydrometridae**

Fig. 186. 2 spp. These delicate bugs walk on all six legs on the water surface and feed on such animals as water-fleas which they spear with the long mouthparts contained in the elongate head.

— Head little, if at all, longer than broad. Eyes close to anterior margin of prothorax 12

12. All legs inserted near the middle of the body (fig. 187). (Ocelli present in winged forms. Antennae with four segments, all of which are roughly equal in thickness)
Mesovelia furcata Mulsant and Rey (MESOVELIIDAE)

Fig. 190. In places where there are floating leaves.

— Legs, particularly hind legs, inserted towards or at the sides of the body (figs. 188 and 189) 13

13. Antennae with five segments, the last three thinner than the first two. Ocelli present. (1·2–2 mm long)
Naeogeidae (Hebridae)

Fig. 191. 2 spp. living among plants at the edge of ponds and lakes.

— Antennae with four segments, all roughly equal in thickness. No ocelli . . . 14

14. Middle legs inserted roughly midway between the fore and hind

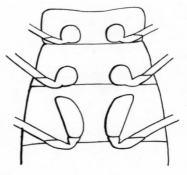

Fig. 187
Underside of *Mesovelia*

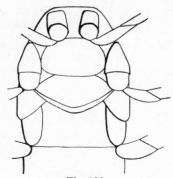

Fig. 188
Underside of *Velia*

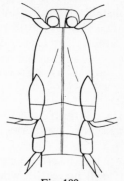

Fig. 189
Underside of *Gerris*

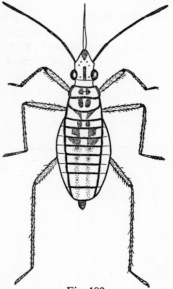

Fig. 190
Mesovelia furcata 3 mm long
(from m.s.)

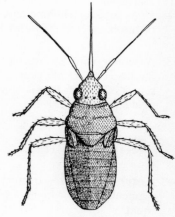

Fig. 191
Naeogeus (Hebrus) ruficeps
(Thomson) 1·3 mm long
(from m.s.)

legs (fig. 188). Hind femora not extending beyond tip of abdomen. 1·5–2·0 mm long *Microvelia* (3 spp.) (fig. 192), 6–8 mm long *Velia* (2 spp.) (fig. 193)

Water-crickets **Veliidae**

Velia is generally found on quiet places of running water. These bugs walk or run over the water surface on six legs.

— Middle legs inserted much nearer hind than fore legs (fig. 189). Hind femora extending well beyond tip of abdomen. 6·5–17 mm long   Pond-skaters or Water-striders **Gerridae**

Fig. 194. 10 spp. *Gerris* supports itself on the tips of the middle and hind legs and progresses across the surface of the water by means of a rowing or occasionally a jumping motion.

15. Head without a sharp, pointed beak (fig. 176). Fore tarsi one-segmented and flat, especially in the males. Scutellum concealed by the hemielytra, except in the minute (1·75–2·5 mm long) *Micronecta.* (fig.195)   .   . **Corixidae**

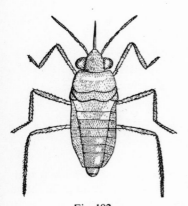

Fig. 192
Microvelia umbricola Wroblewski
1·5 mm long (from m.s.)

Fig. 193
Velia caprai Tamanini 7 mm long
(from m.s.)

Fig. 195. 33 spp. Rapid swimmers like the dytiscid beetles. The males of some species produce a chirp like that of a cricket.

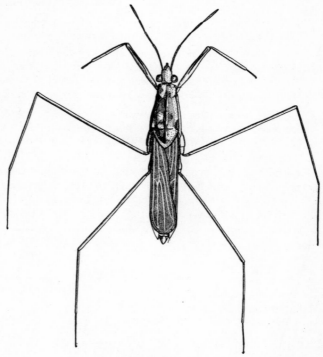

Fig. 194
Gerris lacustris (Linn.) 10 mm long (from m.s.)

— Head with a sharp, pointed beak. Fore tarsi seldom with only one segment, never flat. Scutellum (triangular plate between bases of wings) visible 16

16. Crawling forms with no swimming-hairs on the legs. Two

respiratory tubes (generally held together and appearing as one) at the hind end of the body . . . **Nepidae**

> The Water-scorpion, *Nepa cinerea* Linn. (fig. 196) and Water-stick-insect, *Ranatra linearis* Linn. (fig. 197). Both lurk in thick vegetation in shallow water.

— Swimming forms with a row of hairs down the hind legs. No respiratory tubes . 17

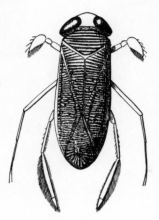

Fig. 195

Corixa falleni (Fieb.) 10 mm long (from m.s.)

17. Flat and broad; swimming back uppermost . . 18

— Boat-shaped; swimming back downwards . . . 19

18. Beak reaching the base of the fore legs when folded under the body. Head broader than long. Fore femur very broad, the tibia folding against it. Winged
Ilyocoris (*Naucoris*) **cimicoides** (Linn.) (NAUCORIDAE)

> Fig. 198. In ponds mainly in southern England.

— Beak reaching the base of the hind legs when folded under the body. Head as broad as long. Fore legs not thus. Usually wingless
Aphelocheirus montandoni Horváth (APHELOCHEIRIDAE)

> Fig. 199. In fast rivers, frequently in the deepest parts. This, having a plastron, is the only bug which does not have to visit the surface for respiratory purposes in the adult stage.

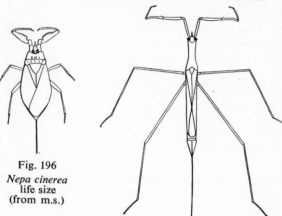

Fig. 196
Nepa cinerea
life size
(from m.s.)

Fig. 197
Ranatra linearis life size (from m.s.)

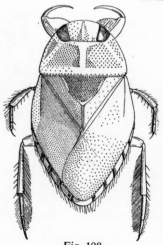

Fig. 198
Ilyocoris cimicoides 10 mm long
(from m.s.)

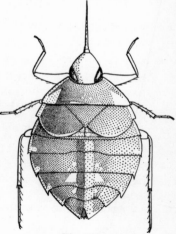

Fig. 199
Aphelocheirus montandoni 8 mm
long (from m.s.)

19. Length 2·5–3 mm. Pronotum and wing-covers sculptured with coarse pits

   Plea leachi MacGreg. and Kirk. (*minutissima* Fuessly) (PLEIDAE)

   Fig. 200. In ponds mainly in southern England.

Fig. 200
Plea leachi 3 mm long
(from m.s.)

— Length 13–16 mm. Pronotum and wing-covers smooth

   Water-boatmen **Notonectidae**

   Fig. 201. 4 spp. of *Notonecta* in still water. Though a powerful swimmer, it spends much of its time at the surface in the position shown in the figure, feeding on terrestrial animals that fall in and aquatic ones that come up for air.

Fig. 201
Notonecta glauca (Linn.) 15 mm
long (from l.s.)

Fig. 202
Parasitic copepod 4 mm long
(from p.s.)

LIVING ON OR IN ANOTHER ANIMAL

It is convenient to include here both true parasites, which derive nourishment from their hosts, and those animals that merely use another to provide shelter, because to the collector an immediate distinction is not always apparent. Separate treatment is advisable because the parasitic habit may lead to degeneration and loss of the features that characterize active members of the group.

All the Sporozoa (Protozoa), all the Trematoda and Cestoda (Platyhelminthes), and many Nematoda, including the horse-hair worms and the rainworms, are parasitic. Form is various and often degenerate to such an extent that morphological features are few; one species may have three hosts and a different form in each, and may pass from one to another in yet a different form; the life-history of all is not known. Full treatment would add to the complexity and length of this work and involve the reader in techniques of which he might not be master, and therefore these groups receive only brief mention.

A number of Sporozoa infest both invertebrate and verte-brate animals. Few are familiar, except for one that causes white spots on fishes. Trematodes are not as degenerate as some parasites, for they still have an alimentary canal, which, as in other Platyhelminthes, has one opening. There is a sucker round this, and another, which is frequently subdivided, may be present on the ventral surface. The gut is bifid and generally with secondary branches. Some trematodes are worm-like, but most are broad and flat. There are two main divisions, the first living on the outside of animals, generally fishes, to which they cling by means of their suckers, and having a simple life-history with only one host, the second living inside and having a complex life-history. A small ciliated miracidium larva emerges from the egg and generally attacks a snail, inside which it turns into a redia. From this somewhat amorphous stage emanate great numbers of cercariae, a form that has been mentioned already. The cercaria of the liver-fluke encysts on vegetation and is eaten by the main host, the sheep, others encyst inside fish and have the main stage inside a fish-eating bird.

The Cestoda, or tapeworms, lack a gut and consist of a number of segments each with a complete set of male and female organs. Typically there is a head or scolex provided with hooks or suckers for attachment, and behind it a growing region perpetually producing segments which drop off when full of mature eggs. Sometimes many thousand segments remain attached, and, as each one is flat, the worm then does resemble a piece of tape, but sometimes there are only three or four segments, and sometimes the segmentation is revealed only by the genital openings. *Diphyllobothrium latum* (Linnaeus) is a parasite of man, inside whose intestines it has been known to reach a length of 45 feet. If the eggs reach water, a round ciliated larva emerges and seeks a *Cyclops*, through whose gut it bores; if the *Cyclops* is later eaten by a pike, the process is repeated and a worm-like larval stage with two characteristic longitudinal grooves at the front end encysts in the flesh. The cycle is completed when man eats uncooked or undercooked fish. Probably the most familiar to the fresh-water biologist is *Schistocephalus gasterostei* (Fabricius), whose life-history is similar. The adult worm infests a fish-eating bird and the stage before that a stickleback, whose sides are frequently seen distended in the most astonishing way by the parasite.

Nematodes have a great variety of ways of life, and may be parasitic or free in any or all stages. A number are to be found in freshwater animals. They have an opening at both ends of the alimentary canal, a hard cuticle and in form are generally elongate with round cross-section (fig. 58).

In the remaining groups parasitism is unknown or confined to a few members. Among the Protozoa the sessile ciliates and suctorians are often attached to animals, sometimes in such numbers that it is difficult to believe that the carrier is not inconvenienced. Some ciliates and rhizopods are internal parasites.

All the Turbellaria are free-living, though one rhabdocoele, *Castradella granea* Braun, lives in the brood-pouch of *Asellus*. Rotifers, like ciliates, frequently settle on animals, and a small number are parasites, a few living inside algae and *Albertia* inhabiting the alimentary canal of oligochaetes.

Members of the family Branchiobdellidae (fig. 59) are true parasites in that they feed on the tissues of the crustaceans to which they attach themselves, but are the only oligochaetes of which this is true. *Chaetogaster limnaei* (fig. 60) is found living free but also in and on snails when apparently it is feeding mainly on cercaria larvae of trematodes. The leeches are one of those groups that trouble the lovers of exact definitions. *Piscicola geometra* (Linnaeus) may be found attached to fish and *Theromyzon tessulatum* (Müller) to the insides of the throats of birds at times when they are not feeding, but also living free; others cling to larger animals only when feeding, and some prey on smaller animals. Where to draw the line at which parasitism stops is a nice point.

Among the Crustacea, the Copepoda are a group in which parasitism has developed several times, and every stage can be found between organisms which are obviously copepods and others whose affinities can be made out only by a study of the young stages. All those in fresh water attack fish, and fig. 202 shows a specimen that has lost nearly all trace of segmentation and appendages, though the paired egg-sacs indicate its copepod relationship. *Argulus* (fig. 77), the fish louse, may, as already mentioned, be found living free or attached to a fish.

The immature stages of Hydrachnellae—little round objects with six legs—are parasitic on a variety of freshwater animals, mainly insects, and some contrive to attach themselves to the adult flying stage. The Unionicolidae infest mussels, and in this family the adults are parasitic too.

The Mollusca lead independent lives, but *Anodonta*, the Swan Mussel, ejects tiny larvae, in which, however, the bivalve structure is apparent, and these attach themselves to fish for a while.

Insect parasites are few in fresh water and known only in two orders. *Agriotypus armatus* Walker is probably the best known of the small number of Hymenoptera that parasitize aquatic animals. The adult swims down into a stream and lays its eggs in the larvae of *Silo* and other caddis species. The naturalist who is not a parasitologist will not be aware of this creature until the caddis has pupated and closed its case with a stone in the usual way. The parasite larva, which destroys its host in the pupal stage, produces a narrow ribbon, often longer than the case, and uses it as a means of obtaining oxygen. This conspicuous object projecting from the case indicates at once that a parasite is within.

Sisyra (fig. 119) lives in and feeds on sponges.

Certain species of chironomid larvae live under the wing cases of Ephemeroptera nymphs or within the rim of the shells of *Ancylus lacustris*, but they appear to gain nothing except shelter from this habit. Sciomyzid larvae may be found inside snail shells, but they are probably more properly regarded as predators than as parasites.

ADDITIONAL REFERENCES

Brindle, A. (1958), Notes on the identification of *Limnophila* larvae, *Trans. Soc. Brit. Ent.* **13**, 57–68 (p. 91).
Brindle, A. (1964), Taxonomic notes on the larvae of British Diptera, 16 and 17. Stratiomyidae. *Entomologist* **97**, 91–96 and 134–139.
Brindle, A. (1964), *ibid*. 18. Empididae. *Entomologist* **97**, 162–165.
Brindle, A. (1958–61), *ibid*. Tipulidae. *Ent. mon. Mag.* **94-97** (9 pts).
Chiswell, J. R. (1956), A taxonomic account of the last in star larvae of some British Tipulinae (Diptera, Tipulidae). *Trans. R. Ent. Soc. Lond.* **108**, 409–484.

INDEX

Where a family name is derived from a generic name also quoted in the text, both are indexed under the generic name, e.g. for Culicidae, see *Culex*. Anglicized names are indexed under the Latin form, e.g. for insects see Insecta.